On Love and Tyranny

On Love and Tyranny

The Life and Politics of Hannah Arendt

Ann Heberlein

Translated from the Swedish by Alice Menzies

ANANSI
INTERNATIONAL

First published as *Arendt: Om kärlek och ondska* in 2020 by Mondial
First published in English in Canada in 2021 and the USA in 2021
by House of Anansi Press Inc.
Published by agreement with Mondial
www.houseofanansi.com

House of Anansi Press is committed to protecting our natural environment.
This book is made of material from well-managed FSC®-certified forests,
recycled materials, and other controlled sources.

House of Anansi Press is a Global Certified Accessible™ (GCA by Benetech)
publisher. The ebook version of this book meets stringent accessibility standards
and is available to students and readers with print disabilities.

25 24 23 22 21 1 2 3 4 5

Library and Archives Canada Cataloguing in Publication

Title: On love and tyranny : the life and politics of Hannah Arendt /
Dr. Ann Heberlein ; translated by Alice Menzies.
Other titles: Arendt. English
Names: Heberlein, Ann, author. | Menzies, Alice, translator.
Description: Translation of: Arendt : om kärlek och ondska.
Identifiers: Canadiana (print) 20200273426 | Canadiana (ebook) 20200273493 |
ISBN 9781487008116 (softcover) |
ISBN 9781487008123 (EPUB) | ISBN 9781487008130 (Kindle)
Subjects: LCSH: Arendt, Hannah, 1906-1975. | LCSH: Political scientists—
Biography. | LCGFT: Biographies.
Classification: LCC JC251.A74 H4313 2021 | DDC 320.5092—dc23

Book design: Alysia Shewchuk
Cover image: Hannah Arendt in 1933, from *Hannah Arendt: For the Love of the World*
by Elisabeth Young-Bruehl / Wikimedia Commons

*House of Anansi Press respectfully acknowledges that the land on which we operate is the
Traditional Territory of many Nations, including the Anishinabeg, the Wendat, and the
Haudenosaunee. It is also the Treaty Lands of the Mississaugas of the Credit.*

 Canada Council
for the Arts
Conseil des Arts
du Canada
 ONTARIO ARTS COUNCIL
CONSEIL DES ARTS DE L'ONTARIO
an Ontario government agency
un organisme du gouvernement de l'Ontario

*We acknowledge for their financial support of our publishing program the Canada Council
for the Arts, the Ontario Arts Council, and the Government of Canada.*

Printed and bound in Canada

MIX
Paper from
responsible sources
FSC
www.fsc.org
FSC® C103567

"If only world history were not so awful,
it would be a joy to live."

—Hannah Arendt, 1952

Contents

Why Hannah Arendt?

"IF HANNAH ARENDT HAD NOT EXISTED," someone once wrote, "it would most certainly be necessary to invent her." The story of Hannah Arendt's life is one of obstacles and victories, light and darkness, setbacks and successes. Born in the early twentieth century, she lived through two world wars and was driven out of both her homeland—Germany—and Europe, to live in exile in the United States. Hannah's life spanned a decisive chapter in the history of the Western world, a time in which the values and ideas of humankind and its worth, of good and evil, guilt and responsibility, were tested and reshaped.

Hannah Arendt is often described as a philosopher, but she herself rejected this label. In an interview broadcast on West German television in 1964, she pushed back against the notion that she belonged "to the circle of philosophers."

"My profession, if one can even speak of it at all, is political theory. I neither feel like a philosopher, nor do I believe that I have been accepted in the circle of philosophers," she explained.

There is a backstory to Hannah's reluctance to be defined as a philosopher. Despite having claimed, as a teenager, to have chosen between studying philosophy or drowning herself, she was deeply disappointed by intellectuals'—in particular the philosophers'—sympathy for and willingness to surrender to the Nazi ideology that swept through Germany in the 1930s. When Hannah fled her homeland, she made a promise to herself never to associate with intellectuals again. She wanted to change the world, but no longer believed in the power of philosophy to do so. Thus Hannah ended her relationship with the realm of theory, and decided to work practically and politically instead.

In the foreword to *Men in Dark Times* (1968), Hannah writes about those rare people who, with their luminosity, intellect, and originality, manage to spread hope and light, even in moments of desperation:

> Even in the darkest of times we have the right to expect some illumination, and that such illumination may well come less from theories and concepts than from the uncertain, flickering, and often weak light that some men and women, in their lives and their works, will kindle under almost all circumstances and shed over the time span that was given them on earth.

There is no doubt that Hannah Arendt herself belonged to the group of people who possessed this singular ability to spread light even in the darkest of times, shining so brightly that their impact is felt long after their time on earth is over.

The letters she exchanged with Martin Heidegger, Heinrich Blücher, Kurt Blumenfeld, Karl Jaspers, Gershom Scholem, and Mary McCarthy paint a picture of a woman with a sharp intellect, a cutting wit, a broad capacity for self-reflection, and a passionate attitude toward the world. This combination of qualities — of heart and mind, common sense and emotion — is exceptional.

Hannah Arendt has been a friend of mine for many years. I first read her as a theology undergraduate at Lund University in the early nineties, and immediately found myself drawn to her style of reasoning and her clear arguments. She awoke my interest in thinkers like Kierkegaard, Jaspers, and Heidegger, and soon became something of an intellectual kinswoman to me. Hannah's discussions of forgiveness proved vital to my doctoral thesis, *Kränkningar och förlåtelse* (Violations and Forgiveness), and she has featured in one way or another in all of my books since.

At some point during my postgraduate studies, I came across Elżbieta Ettinger's book on Hannah's love affair with Martin Heidegger. The book drew my attention to the private Hannah, and I began to devour Hannah

Arendt biographies and the correspondence between Hannah and her friends. The idea of writing a book about Hannah, her life, and her philosophy took root, and I am so pleased that I have finally had the opportunity to do just that.

I make no claim to providing a complete picture of Hannah's life and philosophy; that was never my intention. Instead, I have taken the liberty of focusing on the events in Hannah's life that interest me most, lifting out the ideas I find most fruitful and attempting to place Hannah, her story, and her thinking into a wider context.

Hannah Arendt was not just a brilliant theorist; she was also a fascinating woman who lived a dramatic life. That is what I want to talk about here. My ambition is to depict Hannah's life and development as an intellectual — her thinking is closely related to her concrete experiences, after all — and to outline a dramatic moment in the history of humankind.

Using her own books, essays, and poems, the correspondence sent between Hannah and her many friends, her interviews, and her diary entries, I want to tell the story of Hannah Arendt and the concepts that became major themes in her life: love and evil.

Introduction

That Which Should Never Have Happened

HANNAH'S *DENKTAGEBUCH*, her intellectual diary, contains a reflection on love and evil. Taking the concept of *amor mundi* — love of the world — as her starting point, she muses on the difficulty of loving the world. Why must we do it, and why is it so hard? The love Hannah discusses here is not love in the conventional sense. To love the world means reconciling oneself with it, in all its imperfection and fragility, because this reconciliation is necessary for one's continued existence. For Hannah Arendt, it was a case of understanding and accepting what really happens. How could anyone love the world after the Holocaust? In what kind of world is something like the Holocaust even possible?

Hannah links *amor mundi* to responsibility, reflection, and judgement. It is a love that presupposes contemplation

of one's own actions and an understanding of their conse-
quences. In this approach, we see parallels to her thoughts
on evil. Indifference can, according to Hannah, be fertile
ground for evil, while the opposite of indifference is reflec-
tion. As a result, everyone has a responsibility to reflect
on their own deeds, a responsibility to choose, a respon-
sibility not to simply obey orders and follow the crowd.

Hannah's notion of "the banality of evil," as she came
to call it, aroused strong disgust and anger among the
intellectual circles of the 1960s. Her description of Adolf
Eichmann, one of the architects of the Holocaust, as an
unimaginative bureaucrat who was simply doing his
job, shocked the world. Critics saw Hannah's argument
as a diminishment of Eichmann's guilt, and her book
Eichmann in Jerusalem: A Report on the Banality of Evil (1963)
was lambasted in the press, causing many a friend and
colleague to turn their backs on her.

In the infamous interview with Günter Gaus broad-
cast on West German television just after its publication,
Hannah is asked whether she wishes she had never
written the book. Does she believe that, despite all the
negative reactions, all the hate, she did the right thing
by writing about Eichmann the way she did?

Hannah, a middle-aged woman at the time, listens
to Gaus's question with a frown. She is wearing a dark
dress, and her once-black hair, though thick as ever, is
flecked with grey. She has one leg nonchalantly crossed
over the other, her dark eyes are guarded yet alert, and

she is holding a cigarette in one hand. Gaus seems almost rapt as he waits for her reply.

Hannah leans back in her armchair, studies Gaus, and takes a deep drag on her cigarette before she speaks. Her answer recalls the motto of Holy Roman Emperor Ferdinand I, *fiat iustitia, et pereat mundus* (let justice be done, though the world perish). She raises her free hand and points at Gaus, as though to stress the importance of her words: *Fiat veritas, et pereat mundus*. The truth must be told, regardless of the consequences of that truth. It is a worthy motto for someone who put their life on the line on more than one occasion, in their steadfast belief in what is true and right. Hannah was not, first and foremost, an activist. At that point, she was not even entirely political. She was a scholar, and a scholar's primary driving force is, of course, the search for the truth.

Her studies, first with Martin Heidegger and later with Karl Jaspers, resulted in a doctoral thesis on the concept of love in Saint Augustine's writing, and she may well have continued to explore different forms of love if the era in which she lived had not forced her to confront other human phenomena, such as evil.

In countless articles and several books—among them *Eichmann in Jerusalem*, which is probably her best-known work—Hannah explores the concept of evil, examining its mechanisms, origins, content, and nature. Why do we wrong one another? Why do so few intervene when they witness profound wrongdoing? And how should we

understand the particular type of evil that manifests as anti-Semitism? Hannah's weapon against evil was her intellect, and she attacked it in much the same way she attacked every problem: by analyzing and naming it. In both *The Origins of Totalitarianism* and *On Violence*, as well as in *Responsibility and Judgment*, she examines the expression of evil. Hannah's understanding of the consequences of real atrocity is coloured by having stood face-to-face with what "should never have happened," as she puts it in *Responsibility and Judgment*.

It is a highly effective description of a phenomenon that is both utterly tangible and yet evasive, an attempt to answer a question that cannot be answered, to define what cannot be defined; to grasp something that is forever slipping through our fingers, changing shape and reappearing in the most unexpected of places, in the most unlikely of contexts.

In the television interview with Günter Gaus, Hannah describes her own reaction on learning the true extent of the Nazis' war crimes — the number of dead, the systematic extermination of Jews, the horrors of the concentration camps. Hannah mentions Auschwitz and falls silent, pauses. She takes a sip of water and then slowly lowers the glass, catching her breath before matter-of-factly, exhaustively, explaining to Gaus, who is sitting quietly in the armchair opposite, how the realization gradually dawned on her. The camera zooms in on her face, and in her eyes we see a hint of the shock she describes:

That was in 1943. And at first, we didn't believe it—
although my husband and I always said that we could
expect anything from that bunch. But we didn't believe
this, because militarily it was unnecessary and uncalled
for. My husband is a former military historian, he
understands something about these matters. He said
don't be gullible, don't take these stories at face value.
They can't go that far! And then a half-year later, we
believed it after all, because we had the proof. That
was the real shock. Before that, we said: Well, one has
enemies. That is entirely natural. Why shouldn't a
people have enemies? But this was different. It was as
if an abyss had opened. Because we had the idea that
amends could somehow be made for everything else,
as amends can be made for just about everything at
some point in politics. But not for this. This ought not
to have happened.

And yet it did. How could it have happened? For Hannah,
the issue of the Holocaust was not a theoretical one; the
question of evil was not purely a philosophical problem.
Evil and the Holocaust were very much personal issues—
as might be expected from someone who has been forced
to give up their life, their language, and their community.

But before we begin to unpack her most complex ideas,
let us start from the beginning, with Hannah Arendt's
birth. The year is 1906, and the place is Linden, Hanover.

One

Young Hannah

MARTHA WAS HEAVILY PREGNANT when she bought it: the book that would follow her throughout life, that she would pack every time she moved or fled, from city to city and country to country, across the Atlantic to the United States. She could predict none of this in the fall of 1906, of course, as she carefully picked out the red book with the words *Unser Kind* (Our Child) printed in black type on the cover. The pages between the two red covers were largely blank, waiting to be filled in. Waiting for stories about the baby she was carrying beneath her heart.

The baby in question was much longed for — the Arendts' first and, as it would turn out, only child. Martha Cohn and Paul Arendt were both born and raised in the East Prussian capital, Königsberg, but had left their hometown to study and see the world. Martha had spent

three years in Paris, where she studied French and music, and Paul had visited several of Europe's major cities—he had seen the Parthenon in Athens and the Colosseum in Rome—before training as an engineer at the Albertina, the Königsberg university famous for Immanuel Kant's work there.

Both Paul and Martha came from the affluent Jewish middle class. The Cohns were involved in the import and export of Russian goods, and J. N. Cohn & Co., the company run by Martha's father, Jacob, was Königsberg's largest, one of the most important tea merchants in Europe—supplying, among others, the British with Russian tea. Paul's father, Max Arendt, was a business-man involved in politics in Königsberg.

There were almost 5,000 Jews in Königsberg at the start of the twentieth century, and like Martha's parents, many of them were Russian Jews who had fled pogroms and persecution in their homelands. Jacob Cohn had left Russia in 1852, as a result of Czar Nicholas I's hostile poli-cies. His wife, Fanny Spiero, had a similar story.

Paul Arendt's family also had ties to Russia, but they had arrived in Königsberg much earlier, in the mid-eight-eenth century. The Arendts had left Russia prior to the forced displacement of Jews to the Pale of Settlement— the large area spanning what is now Lithuania, Belarus, and Ukraine in which Jews were permitted to settle, as decreed by Catherine the Great.

Persecution and flight were intrinsic to Martha and

Paul's pasts, and with time they would also become part of their daughter's future. But in the fall of 1906, Martha's thoughts were elsewhere. The world was enjoying a period of relative calm, and the German economy was thriving. Europe had been at peace for decades, and the powerful alliances struck between Germany, Austria-Hungary, and Italy on one side, and France, Russia, and Serbia on the other seemed to guarantee stability long into the future. The anti-Semitism that had forced both the Cohns and the Arendts to flee Russia also seemed to have been consigned to history. The age of the pogrom was over. The future looked bright.

Martha and Paul were young newlyweds, and they had just moved into their first home in the pleasant Hanover suburb of Linden. Martha's thoughts revolved around the child she felt kicking beneath the taut skin of her belly. She had spent all summer and fall devouring books about childhood development, reading up on child psychology and childrearing methods. The Arendts considered themselves to be enlightened, modern people, and they wanted to raise their child to be an independent, free-thinking person. Among Martha's progressive middle-class friends, topics like breastfeeding and toilet training often came up in conversation.

The Arendts had a keen interest in society and politics, and even thought themselves somewhat radical. Both had joined the left-wing Social Democratic Party as teenagers, during a period when the party was still outlawed

in Germany, and they had very little interest in religion. Like war and anti-Semitism, religion seemed to belong to the past. Martha and Paul were modern people who rejected superstition and conservative views of society and its people. To them, there was no question that their child, irrespective of gender, would receive a good education and be well prepared for the world of work. Martha had been unable to pursue further education herself, as women had been barred from studying at the university in Königsberg when she was younger, but in 1906, the same year she gave birth to her daughter, the Albertina finally opened its doors to them.

On October 14, 1906, their little girl came into the world. Her parents gave her the name Johanna, but she would be known as Hannah throughout her life, and she would eventually become one of the twentieth century's most important and influential thinkers. Martha and Paul knew none of this, of course, but like all new parents, they thought their daughter was a miracle. With her pale skin, big eyes, and dark hair, Hannah was like a tiny doll. Her parents gazed at her in wonder, and Martha carefully noted down the girl's measurements in her red book, along with every minor ailment and development the girl experienced.

In the oldest preserved photograph of Hannah, we see a smiling young girl in her grandfather Max's arms. Hannah is just over a year old in the image, and the family is on one of its frequent visits to Königsberg. Max is a tall

man with a neat white beard, and he is holding the little girl tightly but carefully—perhaps to stop her squirming out of his grip. According to Martha's notes in *Unser Kind*, Hannah was a lively girl who began walking and talking before she was even one. A real "sunshine child."

When Hannah was barely four, however, illness darkened the small family's world. The syphilis Paul Arendt had contracted as a young man flared up again, and by 1910 he was so unwell he could no longer work. As a result, he, Martha, and young Hannah moved back to Königsberg, both to be closer to their families and because Paul needed treatment at the university hospital there. The progression of his condition was slow but relentless, and in the summer of 1911, Paul was admitted to hospital. By this point, the syphilis had reached the stage where it caused both physical and psychological symptoms: Hannah's father lost control of his body and his mind. As his spasms increased in intensity, a mild psychosis also took hold.

As a result of her father's illness, Hannah learned from an early age that life is fragile and that death can shatter a person's world at any moment. When her father fell ill, her grandfather Max became her anchor point. Hannah loved going to synagogue with him, and she enjoyed their walks through the city's beautiful parks. Paul and Martha may not have been religious, but Max was very much active within Königsberg's Jewish congregation. Hannah was fascinated by the rituals, and listened

wide-eyed as Grandfather Max welcomed her into his trove of Jewish stories, parables, and myths.

As an adult, Hannah rarely spoke about her childhood. She wrote nothing about her youth and was sparing with details of her early years in interviews. The majority of what we know about Hannah's childhood and teenage years comes from the notes Martha kept in *Unser Kind*. On the few occasions Hannah did speak about her childhood, she often mentioned her grandfather Max as a great storyteller. Perhaps it was Max who sparked her interest in literature? Or was it the well-stocked bookshelves of her childhood home that made Hannah into a reading, writing woman? She always had her nose in a book, and over the course of her youth she read everything—from poetry and fiction to Kant and Greek mythology.

Hannah's beloved grandfather Max passed away in March 1913, followed in October by Paul. In less than a year, young Hannah had lost both her grandfather and her father. Martha was beside herself with grief and worry: how would she and Hannah cope? Though the Arendt and Cohn families were well off and would support both Martha and Hannah, being a widow with a small child was far from easy in the early twentieth century. In a photograph taken not long after Paul's death, we see a pale but composed woman, and a serious young girl with long, plaited hair. Hannah is leaning against her mother, who is sitting down. Both are dressed in dark colours, and

their hands are tightly clasped as though it were them against the world.

Martha did her best to maintain a sense of normality for herself and her young daughter—she taught Hannah to play the piano and made sure the girl saw her relatives regularly. Hannah was particularly enamoured of Paul's stepsister, Frieda, who took her to the beach in the summer and helped Martha by picking her up from kindergarten. Hannah was fond of kindergarten, where she had impressed her teachers with her precocious reading skills, but she was enrolled at the Szittnick School in the fall of 1913 and was even happier there. Martha documented Hannah's enthusiasm and progress in *Unser Kind*, noting with satisfaction that she was a quick learner and that, according to her teacher, Miss Jander, she was a full year ahead of her classmates.

Paul left behind a large collection of books. He had been passionately interested in Greek and Roman mythology, and he had read both Latin and Greek. Hannah threw herself into her father's books, and would come to enjoy great success studying the ancient languages.

THE SUMMER OF 1914 has been described as "Europe's last summer." It was a carefree time full of garden parties and confidence in the future, lazy days on the beach, and wonderful weather. In *The World of Yesterday*, celebrated Austrian Jewish author Stefan Zweig writes,

Even without the disaster it brought down on the whole of Europe, that summer of 1914 would have been unforgettable. I have seldom known a summer more luscious, more beautiful, I am tempted to say more *summery*. The sky was a silken blue day after day, the air was soft and sultry, the meadows warm and fragrant, the woods dark and lush with young green growth. Even today, when I say the word "summer" I instinctively think of the glorious July days that I spent in Baden near Vienna that year.

Martha and Hannah, too, enjoyed that wonderful, sun-drenched season, spending a few months at the Cohn family summer house in the town of Neukuhren (now Pionersky) on the Baltic coast. Dips in the sea were followed by croquet in the garden, and Martha rediscovered some of the peace of mind she had lost when her beloved Paul fell ill and died.

The idyll came to an abrupt end, however. On June 28, news reached the holidaymakers that Franz Ferdinand, the heir to the Austro-Hungarian throne, had been assassinated by a Serbian nationalist in Sarajevo. This proved the starting shot in a fateful diplomatic crisis that culminated in what came to be known as the Black Week.

On July 28, Austria-Hungary declared war on Serbia, and this was soon followed by a number of other declarations of war. The alliances that had been struck between various European countries, intended to guarantee peace

and stability, suddenly demanded action. Russia backed its ally Serbia with an ultimatum sent to Austria-Hungary, warning of military intervention. Three days later, on August 1, Germany declared war on Russia, in support of Austria-Hungary, while France mobilized to aid Russia. In response, Germany declared war on France two days later, and demanded free passage through Belgium, which was refused. On August 4, German troops entered Belgium in order to outflank the French army—an act that moved Britain to declare war on Germany.

Within that short week, the Great War set Europe ablaze—soon to engulf the whole world. Martha and Hannah returned to Königsberg in a panic, but Martha did not feel safe there. She described the final days of August as "terrible days full of worries," knowing that the Russian army was so close. It seemed only a matter of time before the troops would invade East Prussia, and in August, Martha and Hannah fled Königsberg, not knowing whether they would ever be able to return. This would be Hannah's first flight, but far from her last.

THE TRAIN THAT TOOK Hannah and her mother from Königsberg to Berlin was full to bursting with uniformed soldiers and people on the run. The atmosphere was chaotic; there were whispers about torched, plundered villages, and talk of bloodthirsty Cossacks, violence, and death. Martha's younger sister Margarethe lived

with her husband and three children in Berlin, and they took in both Hannah and Martha. In her childish innocence, Hannah was thrilled to be able to spend more time with her cousins, and she was excited about starting at a new school—an all-girls school in Charlottenburg. "Here relatives and strangers give her a lot of love and spoil her," Martha wrote in *Unser Kind*. "Nevertheless, an excessively great yearning remains in her for her home and Königsberg."

Martha was extremely worried, and she nervously followed every development in the war. She and Margarethe huddled over the radio during each news report and devoured newspapers, hoping for the best. The situation seemed hopeless, the war already lost—the Russians were approaching East Prussia from two fronts like an enormous pincer, and with their 400,000 men, their army was twice as strong as the German force desperately trying to hold them back. The German commander, Max von Prittwitz, wanted to retreat, and seemed prepared to sacrifice East Prussia to do so, but the military command responded by replacing him with retired war hero Paul von Hindenburg, who, against all expectations, led the Germans to victory.

Combining past experience with new technology, the Germans managed to outmanoeuvre the Russians: using shortwave radio, they succeeded in intercepting their opponents' plans ahead of the armies meeting at the Battle of Tannenberg between August 24 and 30, 1914,

and were therefore able to outwit them. The Russian army suffered a brutal defeat: 78,000 men were killed, and another 92,000 were taken prisoner. Just a few weeks later, the German army dealt yet another blow to the remaining Russian forces stationed by the Masurian Lakes. The Russians retreated, and East Prussia was liberated.

Hannah and her mother were able to safely move back to Königsberg in November that year, and everyday life slowly began to return. In the shadow of a war that cost millions of people their lives and forever knocked the world off-kilter, Hannah approached her teens. Martha's motherly worries and concerns are all documented in *Unser Kind*: Hannah came down with the measles, had an inexplicably high fever on several occasions, was fitted for braces because of a crooked front tooth, and, in 1915, suffered a long and painful ear infection.

Martha was concerned that her daughter, once so happy and carefree, had become broody and occasionally prone to angry outbursts: "I see my own youth repeated in her and am saddened by that; concerning people, she will follow the same path of tears that I did. But I guess no one can be spared his fate. If only she could be like her father! The Arendts are so much more robust in their feelings and can therefore master life so much more readily than people of our kind," she laments in *Unser Kind*. The closer Hannah came to her teens, the more her brooding, melancholic side seemed to emerge.

She began writing poetry and became engrossed in philosophy and theology. She was particularly fond of the Christian philosophers Søren Kierkegaard and Immanuel Kant—unusual choices for a young girl who had grown up in a non-religious Jewish family.

Though the war never reached Königsberg, Martha and Hannah did suffer hardship. Like the majority of Germans, there were times when they struggled to get hold of food. Thanks to the British navy's highly effective blockade of transport routes to Germany, the situation became critical during 1917 and 1918. All imports of food supplies dried up, and the Germans were forced to survive on what they could grow or produce themselves. Toward the end of the war, Martha's finances also began to dwindle. Her father, Jacob Cohn, had left her a sizable sum of money when he died, but it didn't last forever. Martha had no income of her own, and the family company's activities had all but ground to a halt—it became impossible to import and export goods like tea and confectionery in the midst of a raging war that deployed blockades as a weapon.

As a result, Martha decided to rent out a room in their home. A Jewish student by the name of Käthe Fischer moved in, and she and Hannah soon began to behave broadly like siblings, with both furious arguments and giggling, warm interactions. Käthe was five years older than the twelve-year-old Hannah, and she was quick-witted and intelligent. To Martha's relief, Hannah

seemed to come out of her shell, and melancholy no longer dominated her daughter's moods. Hannah had begun studying Greek by this point, and she was increasingly absorbed by her school work, though her social life was also particularly intense. Hannah had found a group of young Jewish friends, the majority a few years older than her, and despite being the youngest member, she was also the natural centre of the group.

Martha, too, began to look outward, focusing her attention primarily on politics. The home she shared with Hannah became a meeting place for social democrats during both the last two years of the war and the 1918–19 revolution, when German social democrats and communists tried and—though managing to overthrow the monarchy—ultimately failed to achieve a revolution the same way their peers in Russia had the previous year.

The year after the revolution, Martha remarried. She had been close to a widower called Martin Beerwald for several years, and in February 1920 they decided to form a union, moving into his house. Hannah, who was thirteen at the time, gained two older stepsisters—though this was far from a painless experience. With her fiery temper, strong will, dazzling intellect, and constant stream of chatter, Hannah was very different to the quiet Beerwald sisters, Clara and Eva. Both girls were shy, and the hyper-intelligent but highly insecure Clara was plagued by recurring depression. Martha and Martin's marriage was, however, a happy one: Martha became a good source of

support for Martin's daughters, and Martin guaranteed financial security for Martha and Hannah. With Martin by her side, Martha no longer needed to worry about poverty or hunger.

Hannah's teens were characterized by her studies and her intense friendships. She oscillated between being introverted, completely absorbed by books — she was always reading, as her childhood friend Anne Mendelsohn Weil once said — and being talkative and reckless. She was, as her mother Martha put it in *Unser Kind*, *widerborstig*, stubborn and obstinate, which often led to conflict, at home and at school. Hannah was a highly gifted student, but she also had real trouble with authority.

After one of Hannah's teachers insulted her when she was fifteen — exactly what this insult consisted of remains unclear — she decided to boycott his lessons. Being both charismatic and popular, she managed to convince her fellow students to join her boycott, which ultimately led to her expulsion from school. Martha took the highly unusual step of taking her daughter's side in the conflict, and Hannah left the Luise School, where she had been a student for years, for good.

Hannah moved to Berlin, where she spent a year living in a student residence while she studied Greek, Latin, and theology at university. She was not left entirely to her own devices at such a young age, however; Martha had made sure that her social democrat friends, the

Levins, kept a watchful eye over the strong-willed teenager. When Hannah eventually returned to Königsberg, she chose to study for her high school exams on her own, with her beloved Aunt Frieda as an informal supervisor. Martha's good friend Adolf Postelmann was the principal of a boys' school, and took on the formal supervisory duties.

In the spring of 1924, Hannah sat her final exams, a whole year before any of her former classmates. She received a set of small golden medals bearing a portrait of Albert, Duke of Prussia, as proof of passing the exams, and was unable to resist the temptation to put on the medallions and pay a visit to her old school. The message to her old classmates and teachers was clear: her expulsion hadn't hindered her. On the contrary she had done better on her own than her classmates had in school.

Hannah had developed a passionate relationship with language — with words, reading, and writing. She had read extensively in the classical languages and had, as Anne Mendelsohn Weil put it, read "everything." Shortly after her eighteenth birthday, she moved to Marburg to study theology and philosophy. The former may seem a strange choice for a secular, non-practising Jew — why read Christian theology? — but the answer likely comes in the form of Kierkegaard. The Danish Christian existentialist was one of Hannah's great intellectual loves, on a par with the German duty ethicist Immanuel Kant.

But why Marburg? The answer this time is Martin Heidegger. Hannah's first boyfriend, Ernst Grumach, was five years older than her, and had already spent some time studying in Marburg. Hannah listened raptly to his stories about the brilliant professor who was on the verge of revolutionizing German philosophy. After her time in Berlin—a year during which Hannah had gained confidence and independence—she was determined to study philosophy, to understand more about existence, and who better to guide her in that quest than Martin Heidegger, the philosopher everyone was talking about?

So, in 1924, just a few months after passing her final exams with distinction, Hannah did what many other young, intellectual Germans were doing: she travelled to Marburg to hear and learn from Martin Heidegger.

Full of fear and expectation, she left behind Königsberg and her mother—everything she knew and was—and took a Kierkegaardian "leap of faith" into the unknown.

Two

Passion

"THE RUMOR ABOUT HEIDEGGER put it quite simply: Thinking has come to live again; the cultural treasures of the past, believed to be dead, are being made to speak, in the course of which it turns out that they propose things altogether different from the familiar, worn-out trivialities they had been presumed to say. There exists a teacher; one can perhaps learn to think," Hannah Arendt would later write in honour of Martin Heidegger on his eightieth birthday.

Learning to think—what could be more tempting to a young person who once claimed, "I can either study philosophy or I can drown myself"?

For Hannah, meeting Martin became synonymous with her entry into the world of philosophy. Many years later, Hannah would claim that philosophy was her first love, and Martin Heidegger was the physical incarnation

of the discipline. He was The Philosopher personified: brilliant, handsome, poetic, and simply dressed—as though to prove that he was above such worldly concerns as fashion—with a fire in his eye. He was an intellectual, but he was also a man who liked to ski and to walk in the woods. He gave lectures that kept his audience rapt, but he also spent a lot of time alone, in the simple log cabin his wife had had built for him in Todtnauberg.

Martin Heidegger was, in other words, irresistible to a young person with an intellectual hunger and lofty ideals. Young men and women applied to study at Marburg purely because of his post there; the reputation of the university professor who kept alive the flame of Edmund Husserl, the great German Jewish phenomenologist, drew them in.

When Hannah entered Martin's life, he was in the final phase of his great project, the work that earned him a place among the twentieth century's most important philosophers: *Sein und Zeit* (published in English as *Being and Time*). Martin lived a highly conventional life: comfortable and proper, but lonely. "I live in solitude," he wrote in one of his first letters to Hannah, making it clear that he longed for a kindred spirit with whom to share his thoughts. Someone who could listen and keep him company when the solitude became too much; someone who could cure his loneliness.

Hannah's first few years at university coincided with the period of relative calm that the government

of Germany's recently established Weimar Republic managed to achieve through a program intended to stabilize the economy and prevent runaway inflation. Toward the mid-1920s, the economy slowly began to recover from the First World War, and living standards rose for the majority of Germans. Cultural life flourished, and a diverse range of authors including Bertolt Brecht, Ernst Jünger, Thomas Mann, Alfred Döblin, and Erich Maria Remarque rose to prominence. Many German artists and authors turned to expressionism, and life in the capital, Berlin, was hectic and decadent.

Christopher Isherwood's novel *Goodbye to Berlin*—like Josef von Sternberg's film *The Blue Angel*, featuring Marlene Dietrich in the lead role as a vampy nightclub singer called Lola Lola—depicts this almost mythical period in Berlin, one dominated by both euphoria and a sense of impending doom. The German film industry enjoyed a golden era, with movies like Fritz Lang's *Metropolis*, and, in 1929, the first German sound film, *Melody of the World*, being released. Alcohol flowed freely, the club scene was intense, and sexuality was loose; the mood was both exhilarated and nostalgic, the people unscrupulous.

Marburg, a small university town in the state of Hessen, was nowhere near as decadent as the capital. In her autobiography, Hannah Tillich, who was married to Paul Tillich, a professor of systematic theology at the university in the 1920s, wrote that bobbed hair and fashionable clothes still drew disapproving looks from

strangers on the street. A certain conservatism held sway in Marburg, despite the fact that the town was also home to an intellectual revolution, with a new way of thinking dominating the academic circles there. Students from across Germany applied to join Martin Heidegger's seminars and listen to his groundbreaking lectures. It was Heidegger, an apprentice of Edmund Husserl, who created modern continental philosophy, and Marburg is where it took root.

Despite the conservatism of the small town and the occasionally stifling narrow-mindedness of its inhabitants, it is easy to see how Hannah—a reading, thinking, eager young woman—allowed herself to be influenced by the more decadent trends from fashionable Berlin. She had an intellectual, inquisitive approach to life, as well as a sense of melancholy that comes through in the poetry she wrote in the early 1920s.

During her time in Marburg (1924–26) and later Heidelberg (1926–29), Hannah both read and wrote a lot of poetry—poetry that often focused on life's impermanence, the longing for a diffuse *you*, and the search for the self. When she arrived in Marburg, she was young and romantic. She had read Kierkegaard, Goethe, and Thomas Mann. Both Kierkegaard's existentialism and his unhappy relationship with Regine Olsen made a deep impression on Hannah, as did Goethe's classic novel about the sorrows of young Werther. She had devoured Mann's *The Magic Mountain*.

But what visions of love did Hannah encounter in these works? Kierkegaard, Goethe, and Mann all present an image of love that oscillates between great joy and deep sorrow — though mostly sorrow. Love seems to consist largely of suffering, of longing, and of distance. Kierkegaard loves Regine, but for unfathomable reasons he is unable to live with her. Young Werther suffers a deep depression as a result of his unrequited love for Lotte, and ultimately commits suicide. In *The Magic Mountain*, sickly Hans Castorp finds no great joy. During his seven-year stay at the Berghof sanatorium in Davos, he falls head over heels for Clavdia Chauchat. On a literary and theoretical level, Hannah was ready to experience passion in its most destructive form.

In Marburg, she met Martin. Considerably older, with an intense gaze and a dominant presence, he was known as the Magician of Messkirch by his students for his ability to bewitch his audience. And Hannah fell under his spell. She was struck down by a passion, possibly even obsession, that would never fade.

For his part, Martin noticed the slender young woman with dark eyes and thick hair the moment she stepped into his lecture theatre — she was unlike the shapely blonde women he had grown up with, and completely different from the Brunhildesque Elfriede he had married. For weeks, Martin sought out Hannah's gaze across the room, and after almost two months of intense eye contact, he finally invited her to his office. Hannah

arrived in a raincoat, her hat pulled down over her dark hair. She listened to him with downcast eyes, saying nothing but *yes* and *no*, likely paralyzed with nerves and reverence for the great professor.

Hannah's budding femininity and shy manner clearly made a great impression on Heidegger, because he returned to that first meeting in his office several times in the many letters he wrote to Hannah over the years — letters that Hannah carefully saved and preserved. Despite the fact that her life was uprooted several times, when she had to flee Germany first and later France; despite the fact she was interned during the war and lived in exile for many years without a place to call home, she managed to save the letters he wrote to her. Martin, on the other hand, did not save a single letter from Hannah. The only letters of hers that are preserved are those she herself chose to make copies of.

This makes reading their correspondence a strange experience. We see Hannah through Martin's eyes, hear his version of their relationship, read his views on the nature of love and the essence of woman. We can only guess what Hannah wrote in reply. Why did Martin fail to save the letters from the young woman he was so fascinated by? Perhaps he was afraid his wife would find them. Perhaps he simply didn't think that Hannah's letters were important enough to save.

It is clear Martin was as captivated by Hannah as she was by him: "Dear Hannah!" he wrote on November 27, 1925.

"The demonic struck me. The silent prayer of your beloved hands and your shining brow enveloped it in womanly transfiguration. Nothing like it has ever happened to me," he announced with a dramatic flourish.

The impression we get is that their meeting was equally disconcerting for both Hannah and Martin. Hannah — or rather, his strong feelings for Hannah — brought anxiety to Martin's previously ordered life, and he put both his marriage and career at risk by embarking on a relationship with the young student, who also happened to be Jewish — soon to be a taboo.

Hannah, on the other hand, found herself on an emotional rollercoaster that continued for years. At times, Martin made her feel intense joy, and at others, intense despair. "I would have lost my right to live had I lost my love for you," she wrote to him in 1928. As though her life were dependent on his.

In *De la séduction*, French sociologist Jean Baudrillard describes seduction and infatuation using terms that sound almost like a diagnosis, a psychosis — possibly even a delusion. He argues that seduction both aims for and leads to a diminished grasp on reality, blurring the boundaries between the self and the other. This doesn't sound particularly positive, and Hannah's infatuation with Martin certainly wasn't pleasant at all times. Judging by the letters we have access to and the descriptions within, her relationship with Martin seems to have been incredibly painful. Was it love, or was it

dependency? Could it have been a shared madness?

Romantic love is often described as a kind of madness, at least in the world of fiction. In the classic romance novel, love is eternal, absolute, and exclusive; it is the only thing that can bring meaning to life and make existence bearable. It is full of fierce arguments, violent jealousy, wonderful reunions, bitter sorrow, and cruel, sudden deaths. Romeo couldn't live without his Juliet; Bella is prepared to give up her human life for Edward. Anna Karenina throws herself in front of a train when Count Vronsky abandons her. What do these acts represent if not the specific kind of madness caused by desperation?

Perhaps this notion of romantic love in fiction has more to do with an idea of femininity as the force that keeps destructive masculinity in check, of femininity as self-effacing goodness. Sonya Marmeladova, the quiet, self-sacrificing young woman in Dostoyevsky's *Crime and Punishment*, turns to prostitution in order to support her half-siblings and her evil stepmother, and she falls in love with the murderer Raskolnikov. She urges him to confess and takes on his despair, housing his confession and guilt without judgement.

Dostoyevsky, of course, was fixated on trying to describe goodness. There is a Christ figure in each of his novels, and in *Crime and Punishment* it is Sonya who personifies divine goodness. She sacrifices herself for another — for Raskolnikov. Without demanding anything in return, she gives her time, her love, and her

presence. Sonya listens to Raskolnikov the way Hannah listened to Martin. The caring, self-effacing woman is a cultural archetype, a role available to women to play and men to exploit.

The first letters Martin sent to Hannah, in the winter and spring of 1925, are lofty and urgent, chivalrous yet driven, full of descriptions of her. He writes about her "innermost womanly essence" in romantic terms. In his second-ever letter to her, dated February 1925, he writes the following on love:

> Here, being close is a matter of being at the greatest distance from the other — distance that lets nothing blur — but instead puts the "thou" into the mere presence — transparent but incomprehensible — of a revelation. The other's presence suddenly breaks into our life — no soul can come to terms with that. A human fate gives itself over to another human fate, and the duty of pure love is to keep this giving as alive as it was on the first day.

Martin enjoyed admiration and respect not just from his students, but from his colleagues, too. In his letters to Hannah, he talked about his conversations with Edmund Husserl and Rudolf Bultmann, Karl Jaspers and Ernst Cassirer. He gave her access to worlds that had not yet become hers, discussing philosophical thoughts and asking her to read his texts.

"Amo means *volo, ut sis*...I love you—I want you to be what you are," Martin wrote to Hannah. The quote, attributed to Saint Augustine, is an invocation, as though he is creating her through his love. His will brings about her very existence. It must have been overwhelming for a naive eighteen-year-old, and Hannah quickly became the female companion he was looking for—a soulmate, a muse, someone to worship and be worshipped by; a Regine Olsen, a Lotte, a Clavdia Chauchat.

Martin's letters are a study in seduction. At its most basic, seduction is about identifying another person's hopes and dreams and transforming yourself into what they have been fantasizing about. He became the great tortured thinker she dreamed of, and she became the female being—both in body and mind—that he in turn longed for: submissive yet strong, passionate yet sensible, intelligent yet inexperienced.

In love's focus on the other, there is an equal focus on the self. The lovers reflect themselves in each other, searching for both similarities and differences, and hoping and expecting to be understood on a fundamental level.

Just a few weeks into their correspondence, in April 1925, Hannah sent a longer text to Martin, one she called "Die Schatten" (The Shadows), likely a reference or possibly even a reply to one of his arguments, forming its basis in the concept of "the shadows."

Hannah's text is full of references to Martin's conceptual world and his struggle with phenomenology. Like

him, she takes her own existence as her starting point, and makes philosophy from her own experiences. She describes the difficulty of understanding existence, of seeing Being and existence itself. She is a stranger even to herself, but she understands the importance of the shadows. As a result of the shadows that obscure our view of existence, we do, at least, understand that we do not understand.

The text is a philosophical argument, but it also gives us an insight into young Hannah's inner world. She describes herself as vulnerable and afraid, melancholic and alone, but also as passionate and devoted. She writes about a *starre Hingegebenheit an ein Einziges* — a rigid devotion to one thing. What this "one thing" is, whether it refers to Martin, to philosophy, or to something else, remains unclear, but one interpretation is that it is Hannah's way of awarding Martin, or his thinking, her complete loyalty and devotion.

He thanks her for letting him read what he calls her "diary," and describes how important she is to him:

> Since I read your diary, I can no longer say "you don't understand that." You sense it, you — and follow along. There are "shadows" only where there is *sun*. And that is the foundation of your soul. You come straight from the center of your existence to be close to me, and you have become a force that will influence my life forever. Fragmentation and despair will never yield anything like your supportive love in my work.

Martin's reply is an acknowledgement of her intellectual abilities; she understands his thinking. It is also an acknowledgement of how important she is to him. In the same letter, Martin writes that "you will live in my work from now on."

Martin Heidegger's influence over Hannah Arendt's thinking is often emphasized, yet the influence she clearly exerted over him and his thinking is mentioned far less frequently. Martin gave Hannah access to new worlds — he spoke about Socrates, about Plato and Heraclitus; he gave long lectures on literature, music, and poetry. Hannah absorbed this knowledge and thoroughly enjoyed listening to a man who shared the same passion for understanding the order of things as she did — a man who, because of his age and profession, knew far more about it.

And yet, she gave him something in return: she was able to look at things that had become familiar to him with fresh, unclouded eyes.

THE RELATIONSHIP BETWEEN MARTIN and Hannah was, without doubt, imbalanced. They met whenever he had time; Hannah made herself available to him whenever he was able to escape his wife.

Power is an underlying condition in all relationships. To love puts a person in a weak position. There is a temptation to exploit the other person's devotion in order to gain

the upper hand—after all, the person who loves most, who is most dependent, is always in the more vulnerable position. As a result, it is easy, too easy, perhaps, to conclude that Hannah was subordinate and that Martin held the balance of power in their relationship. In all likelihood, the reality was more complex than that.

Power, writes German sociologist Max Weber, is the ability to make things happen—something Hannah certainly had a knack for with Martin. The letters Martin wrote to Hannah, particularly during the first few years of their relationship, demonstrate that he felt a great need for her. Like a young boy seeking his mother's praise, Martin sought Hannah's appreciation. His letters also reveal a powerful sense of yearning for her. In late May 1925, for example, he wrote, "my longing for you is becoming less and less controllable."

Their pining for one another was, to all appearances, mutual, even if Martin's life circumstances did dictate that he was the one who decided if and when they met.

Hannah submitted to his rules, rushing over to see him whenever he sent for her. She even accepted his system of light signals: if the lamp in his window was lit, it meant that he had, for some reason, been forced to cancel their meeting, and she would have to turn around and head home. During the first year of their relationship, they met in her student room and his office. They went on late-night walks, huddled together in dark parks, and spent many an hour on dimly lit benches.

Hannah's time in Marburg, and her secret relationship with Martin, left her isolated and lonely. There was only one other Jewish student in Heidegger's seminar, and he and Hannah grew close. Hans Jonas was one of the few people Hannah invited back to her small attic room, and years later, in a letter, he recalled an episode from one of his visits there. A tiny mouse had taken up residence, and she described the creature as just as lonely — *"so allein"* — as she was.

The love shared by Hannah and Martin was tinged with fear, both of being found out and of the other suddenly disappearing. Neither could place any demands on the other; neither had a right to the other. Their relationship existed solely in the shadows: never acknowledged, never visible.

Hannah wrote her doctoral thesis on Saint Augustine and his concept of love during the period when her relationship with Martin was at its most intense. Taking Augustine's concept of *appetitus*, or craving, as a metaphor for love, Hannah discusses the relationship between love, desire, and fear: "Craving, or love, is a human being's possibility of gaining possession of the good that will make him happy, that is, of gaining possession of what is most his own. That love can turn into fear... Craving, as the will to have and to hold, gives rise in the moment of possession to a fear of losing."

This could easily be a description of her love for Martin. The desire to possess is a key ingredient in

every love affair. It's common to say "my" husband or boyfriend, "my" wife or girlfriend. Even Marcel Proust writes about the urge to possess in *In Search of Lost Time*: "The possession of what we love is an even greater joy than love itself."

It may be that possession, as indicated by Augustine's concept of *appetitus*, is the very essence of passionate love, of love as desire; we want to own the things we crave. Hannah was never able to call Martin her partner because she possessed him for brief intervals only, and the fear of losing him was ever-present.

Three

Limit Situations

AFTER HANNAH LEFT MARBURG to work on her doctoral thesis in Heidelberg, her relationship with Martin continued, and they began meeting in hotels along the railway line between the two towns. "So you aren't coming now — I think I understand," a despairing Hannah wrote to Martin on April 22, 1928, after several days of waiting. Martin, who was visiting Heidelberg at the time, had written to her on April 18, saying: "If I do not visit you this afternoon between two and four, please expect me this evening at 10 o'clock in front of the University library."

How long did Hannah stand outside the library before she realized he would not be coming? Anyone who has ever waited in vain for someone they love will recognize the conflicting feelings that race through your mind as the minutes become hours; the realization that he, your

beloved, is not coming is impossible to ignore — the fear, anger, sorrow, frustration, and despair all too tangible.

That letter Hannah sent Martin on April 22 is one written by a crushed but feverishly infatuated woman:

> What I want to tell you now is nothing but, at heart, a very frank assessment of the situation. I love you as I did on the first day — you know that, and I have always known it, even before this reunion. The path you showed me is longer and more difficult than I thought. It requires a long life in its entirety. The solitude of this path is self-chosen and is the only way of living given to me.

Now twenty-one, Hannah bravely explained to the man she loved, the man who had let her down, that her loneliness was something she had chosen, and that she was grateful to him for showing her the path she had to take.

Many years later, in May 1960, Hannah wrote to her friend Mary McCarthy, who was embroiled in her own passionate love affair with a married man, that she was afraid Mary would end up getting hurt. She begged her friend to be careful, perhaps because of her own bitter experience. Mary replied honestly in a letter from Rome. "Do not worry about me. I *got* hurt, this time," she wrote, going on to describe how a sense of tranquility had returned to her. Hannah replied laconically, perhaps even with a sense of disillusion, that pain "is only another way of being alive."

Hannah's remark that pain is part of life—a way to feel alive—is reminiscent of psychiatrist and philosopher Karl Jaspers's *Grenzsituation*, or limit situation, a concept he defines as a critical existential moment, an instant of psychological challenge seen in the type of major, decisive life events that cannot be avoided. Limit situations are paradoxical in that they make us both see the constraints of life and think of ourselves as intensely alive. Our engagement with life, with our own existence, grows as we learn and accept our own limitations—our mortality, if you like. Death is, without doubt, the ultimate boundary of existence that we must all relate to. It is dizzying to see and feel our limits, while at the same time grasping the importance of life, what we have right here and now.

The letter Hannah wrote to Martin in April 1928 oozes with a sense of limit situation. Faced with her own inability to arouse her beloved's love, she expresses an insight into her own life and the path she must take. Perhaps she realized something decisive about her own existence and the conditions of human life once she acknowledged and accepted Martin's faults? The fact she made a copy of this letter—and kept it until her death—suggests she believed she had reached some kind of decisive moment that day. Perhaps she kept it in order to remind herself of the pain? In order to be able to smile tenderly at young Hannah's despair, safe in the knowledge that her life did not become the lonely wandering she imagined that day in Heidelberg?

THE MOVE TO HEIDELBERG provided Hannah with an intellectual context she had been lacking in Marburg. Her new supervisor there was Karl Jaspers, who had begun his academic career as a psychiatrist and made the switch to philosophy in his forties. Karl and Hannah shared a number of influences — Kant, Kierkegaard, Goethe, and Nietzsche — and were both intellectually indebted to Martin Heidegger. They became friends for life.

In Heidelberg, Hannah also struck up friendships within a larger group of undergraduate and postgraduate students around her own age. She had a number of brief love affairs — with Erwin Loewenson, who later became an author, and with Benno von Wiese, who introduced her to Heidelberg's intellectual salons. Von Wiese, who had just published a study on the German poet and philologist Friedrich Schlegel when he first met Hannah, was considered something of an intellectual superstar, and he and Hannah made a dazzling couple: young, good-looking, and brilliant.

Though Hannah lived an intense, exciting, and stimulating life in Heidelberg, she never forgot Martin. They continued to exchange letters and took the opportunity to meet up whenever they could. In the correspondence from Martin that Hannah preserved, he swears his love to her, writing that he was pleased to see her radiating happiness when they met, and asks her to send him photographs. Many years later, Hannah would openly admit that Martin was the sole reason she had left Marburg.

She needed to break free from him, and she did manage to—but only partly. No one was ever able to fully replace him in her life.

IN 1929, HANNAH TOOK the drastic step of marrying Günther Stern, another of Martin Heidegger's young students. Having first met at university, they became reacquainted at a masquerade ball in Berlin, organized to raise money for a minor Marxist magazine. The ball was held at the Ethnological Museum, and the guests were all dressed for the occasion. Hannah arrived in costume as an Arabian odalisque, and she spent all evening with Günther. Barely a month after the masquerade ball, they moved into a Berlin apartment together.

Like Hannah, Stern came from the assimilated, intellectual Jewish middle class. They moved in the same circles, enjoyed music and literature, and had similar ambitions in life—yet their marriage was never truly happy. Hannah was still in love with Martin, with whom she had kept up contact, despite everything, but Günther had already begun to lose faith in his former idol, concerned by Martin's increasingly reactionary political opinions and violent nationalism.

His misgivings had grown after a visit to the Heideggers' cabin in Todtnauberg. Martin's wife, the blonde Valkyrie Elfriede, had expressed her appreciation for Günther's physique, telling him he should join

the National Socialists. Günther later told Hannah that he had been taken aback by her remarks, and had said to Elfriede, "Look at me and you will see that I belong to those you want to do away with." Elfriede, who had become a member of the National Socialist Party very early on, had not realized that Günther Stern was one of the very people she considered inferior: a Jew.

Despite her new husband's doubts about Martin's views, Hannah persevered in her loyalty and love. Günther continued in blissful ignorance of his wife's relationship with Heidegger, and likely would not have appreciated the letter she sent to Martin in the spring of 1929, shortly after she and Günther became a couple: "Do not forget me, and do not forget how much and how deeply I know that our love has become the blessing of my life." She ends the letter with the affectionate words: "I kiss your brow and eyes."

THE LAST TIME HANNAH saw Martin before she broke off all contact with him and fled Germany was the day after he paid a visit to her and Günther in Berlin. The two men were taking the train to Freiburg together, and Hannah went down to the station to catch one last glimpse of her beloved—Martin Heidegger, not her new husband. The meeting at the station did not go as planned, however, and she became panic-stricken when she realized he did not recognize her:

I had already stood before you for a few seconds, you
had actually already seen me — you had briefly looked
up. And you did not recognize me. When I was a small
child, that was the way my mother once stupidly and
playfully frightened me. I had read the fairy tale about
Dwarf Nose, whose nose gets so long nobody recog-
nizes him anymore. My mother pretended that had
happened to me. I still vividly recall the blind terror
with which I kept crying: but I am your child, I am
your Hannah. That is what it was like today. And then
when the train was about to leave. And it was just as
I had imagined moments before, and so, it seems, had
wanted: you two up there and me alone, completely
powerless. As always, nothing was left for me but to
let it happen, and wait, wait, wait.

Hannah never got a reply from Martin, or at least not
in a letter that she kept. Following his visit to Berlin, all
contact between Hannah and Martin ceased, as far as we
know, until 1933.

IN 1929, THE SAME YEAR Hannah presented her thesis
and married Günther, the stock market crashed in New
York. On Thursday, October 24 — Black Thursday, as it
came to be known — when the market took a dramatic,
unexpected downturn, Hannah had just turned twenty-
three. The crisis quickly hit the American banks, and

though officials began working around the clock, the chaos continued. Photographs and films showing exhausted workers sleeping on the marble floors of the stock exchange soon reached Europe.

During the most intense weeks of the crash, between September 3 and November 13, the industrial stock index fell by 50 percent, meaning that people lost huge sums of money. Hundreds of thousands of people in America were left without jobs, some even losing their homes, and the number of deaths by suicide rose. European newspapers described how destitute stockbrokers, bankers, and ruined millionaires had begun to throw themselves from the skyscrapers on Wall Street in desperation.

In reality, things weren't quite so dramatic—between October 24 and the end of the year, the *New York Times* reported around one hundred suicides and attempted suicides, half of which were said to be linked to the stock market crash. Yet the crash on Wall Street represented the start of a global depression that also had an impact on Europe. Germany—still struggling with the unfavourable terms of the Treaty of Versailles, which had ended the First World War and required the payment of onerous reparations—was hit particularly hard, and since American investments had been vital to the country's boom during the 1920s, the consequences of the crash proved severe.

The early 1930s saw high inflation, unemployment, and social anxiety in Hannah Arendt's homeland,

accompanied by violent riots and fighting in the streets. The established parties, conservative and liberal alike, lost the support of the voters, and the ground was slowly but surely prepared for the National Socialist German Workers' Party (NSDAP), better known as the Nazi Party, to seize power. The Hannah we see in pictures from the late 1920s—her dark hair parted in the centre, and with a romantic, faraway look in her eye that seems to capture the spirit of the times—reached adulthood at an anxious moment in modern history.

In January 1933, when Adolf Hitler was appointed chancellor, life changed fundamentally. "Indifference was no longer possible in 1933," Hannah later explained in an interview. As early as 1931, she had been convinced that the Nazis would one day take over, but few of her friends had been willing to acknowledge where she believed Nazism was heading.

After almost ten years of studying theology and philosophy, Hannah Arendt emerged to face the world. She was concerned by the path Germany seemed to be taking, and her restlessness and fears continued to grow. Philosophy was unable to help her understand what was happening, nor did it seem to be the answer to how the destructive developments could be stopped. She longed for action, and to do something concrete. Something other than thinking.

Four

The Noose Tightens

HANNAH AND GÜNTHER'S MARRIAGE was not quite as harmonious as they may have hoped. Despite coming from similar backgrounds and sharing a range of intellectual interests, their life together was characterized by irritation and arguments. Their differing temperaments caused problems, and the external pressures of living in Germany—the anti-Semitism, political anxiety, and faltering economy—did not help. While hardship and suffering bring some couples closer together, others find themselves torn apart when faced with challenges. Hannah and Günther belonged to the latter group.

Life in Germany was becoming increasingly difficult for the Jewish population, and in 1933 Günther was forced to leave the country. His work with the playwright Bertolt Brecht, a staunch communist, had caught the attention of the authorities, and he escaped to Paris in

fear of his life. Hannah herself remained in Germany, despite the fact that it was an increasingly unsustainable place to live. This dealt the death blow to their marriage, though Hannah and Günther would remain friends for the rest of their lives.

IN EARLY 1933, alarming rumours about Martin's behaviour at the University of Freiburg began to reach Hannah. There were reports that Heidegger, who had recently been appointed rector there, had begun to bar Jewish students from their seminars, to rebuff Jewish doctoral students, and to fail to greet his Jewish colleagues. The news left Hannah dismayed. Though she knew Martin was a member of the Nazi Party, she had never thought of him as an anti-Semite.

Hannah wrote to Martin demanding answers. She wanted to know whether the rumours were true — whether he had been treating Jewish students and fellow staff unfairly.

Reading his response leaves a bitter taste in the mouth. Martin dismisses her questions about his behaviour toward Jewish students, doctoral candidates, and colleagues as being rooted in "a malicious piece of gossip." He writes angrily that he has "long since given up expecting any sort of gratitude or even just decency from so-called 'disciples,'" and ends the letter by assuring Hannah that none of this has anything to do with his

relationship with her. His letter, at times self-pitying, at times aggressive, failed to convince Hannah.

Karl Jaspers, Hannah's supervisor in Heidelberg, was one of those who later suffered during Martin's time as rector. Karl was a lecturer at Heidelberg University, and he also happened to be married to a Jewish woman, Gertrud Mayer. This union caused him huge problems in Nazi Germany. In 1937, he was stripped of the right to teach in German universities, and in 1938, he was forbidden from teaching at all. Until the end of the war, the Jasperses lived in constant fear of being sent to one of the concentration camps.

Karl had first met Martin in the 1920s, when both men were invited to the home of another philosopher (and one of Martin's most eminent mentors), Edmund Husserl. They struck up an immediate rapport, and the intense discussions that began over dinner that evening would continue for years. Karl considered Martin his only equal within the world of philosophy — both men were important figures in the new school of German philosophy that emerged during the 1920s — and in countless letters, long walks, salons, dining rooms, and seminars, they discussed the philosophical questions that engaged them both. They also happened to be good friends — or so Karl Jaspers thought.

But during Martin's last visit to the Jasperses' home, his behaviour toward Karl's wife was utterly shameless. When Karl mentioned that Gertrud had been brought to

tears by the news she had read in the paper, Martin coolly replied that "it makes one feel better to cry sometimes." Following this outburst, Martin left without even saying goodbye to Gertrud.

Despite this behaviour, Karl continued to write to Martin, inviting him back to his home—an offer Martin did not even condescend to reply to.

Years later, when Karl told Hannah about Martin's reprehensible behaviour toward Gertrud, Hannah fiercely defended Martin. The whole thing, she argued, was surely a misunderstanding. There was no way Martin would refuse to speak to Gertrud simply because she was Jewish. Her firm belief in Martin's benevolent attitude toward Jews was bewildering, not least to Karl, who had no idea that she and Martin had been carrying on an affair for years.

During the spring of 1933, Hannah's situation became increasingly desperate, and yet—as she later revealed in an interview—she was perplexed by the reactions of people around her: "The problem, the personal problem, was not what our enemies did but what our friends did. In the wave of *Gleichschaltung* [co-ordination], which was relatively voluntary—in any case, not under the pressure of terror—it was as if an empty space formed around me."

Those who fell into line were not all Nazi sympathizers. Many of Hannah's friends did too, despite the fact that *Gleichschaltung*—the process by which the Nazi

Party took control of all aspects of German society—was, as she explained, at first voluntary. Their acceptance of the new political climate was not necessarily due to conviction alone; the fear of being wronged likely also played a part—an attempt to shore up their own position or possibly even gain a new post.

AFTER GÜNTHER'S ESCAPE FROM Germany, Hannah lived alone in Berlin. She scraped together a living by writing columns and essays for *Frankfurter Zeitung* and *Kölnische Zeitung*, among others, and was awarded a grant that enabled her to write a book about Rahel Varnhagen, a Jewish woman who had been at the centre of a group of intellectuals in eighteenth-century Berlin.

If Hannah's time in Heidelberg had been characterized by lively discussions, scholarly disagreements, and philosophical hair-splitting, her years in Berlin were marked by a sense that the situation was grave. The carefree atmosphere had been replaced by anxiety about the future.

Hannah had become part of a circle of intellectuals, some of whom were politically active on the left or who held anarchist sympathies. Many were toying with the idea of leaving Germany, and they spent their evenings discussing escape plans; as they opened bottles of wine, cigarette smoke hanging thick in the air, they discussed more or less feasible ways of showing resistance. Fear

spilled into every home and bar they frequented. The situation was tense, and most were aware that not only did the regime disapprove of those with Jewish heritage, it was also hostile toward political dissidents, Marxists, and anarchists. How much longer would Hannah and her friends be safe in Germany?

After attending a lecture organized by the Zionistische Vereinigung für Deutschland (the Zionist Federation of Germany), Hannah was left deeply affected by what she heard. The organization's spokesman was Kurt Blumenfeld, a confident, sophisticated man twenty or so years Hannah's senior. He appreciated her intellect and independence, and, on one occasion, gave her a box of Cuban cigars—to her great joy and others' dismay, she smoked them openly, which was uncommon behaviour for a woman at the time. Despite the fact that Hannah did not consider herself a Zionist, she devoted herself to the Zionist movement, and Kurt quickly became a close friend.

Kurt Blumenfeld would prove instrumental in Hannah's understanding of herself as a Jew, as well as in her political awakening. During the 1930s, her engagement became an expression of solidarity with the Jewish heritage she had previously neglected. Years later, in 1963, Hannah wrote about her political background in an open letter to her friend, the Jewish mystic Gershom Scholem:

I am not one of the "intellectuals who come from the German left." You could not have known this, since we did not know each other when we were young. It is a fact of which I am in no way particularly proud and which I am somewhat reluctant to emphasize — especially since the McCarthy era [in the United States]. I came late to an understanding of Marx's importance because I was interested neither in history nor in politics when I was young. If I can be said to "have come from anywhere," it is from the tradition of German philosophy.

Hannah's resistance, in other words, had very little to do with political ideology. Her resistance was not as either a social democrat or a communist, but as a Jew. "If one is attacked as a Jew, one must defend oneself as a Jew. Not as a German, not as a world citizen, not as an upholder of the Rights of Man, or whatever. But: what can I specifically do as a Jew?" she explained in her 1964 interview with Günter Gaus.

THE BURNING OF THE REICHSTAG, the German parliament building in Berlin, on February 27, 1933, is seen by many as precipitating the death blow to German democracy. Hitler took full advantage of the arson attack on the seat of government by an alleged communist to drive through his politics, and the resulting events saw

all political parties but the NSDAP banned. For Hannah, the Reichstag fire represented the moment action became necessary. It was no longer possible to be a passive observer.

After Hitler's rise to power, the process of *Gleichschaltung* was launched. A number of laws were voted through immediately after the elections in March, with the ultimate aim of achieving totalitarian control of Germany and its citizens. Nazi values were promoted as the government took over the media, culture, unions, and schools. Similarly, existing organizations, youth associations, and other groups were transformed into specifically Nazi organizations.

In *The Origins of Totalitarianism*, Hannah describes the totalitarian vision as the urge to "organize the infinite plurality and differentiation of human beings as if all humanity were just one individual." She considered propaganda a necessary part of creating and maintaining a totalitarian state. Indeed, as she wrote: "Only the mob and the elite can be attracted by the momentum of totalitarianism itself; the masses have to be won by propaganda."

Parallel to the government taking control of the people through indoctrination and propaganda, a number of anti-Jewish laws were passed, one after another, limiting the Jewish population's ability to participate in German society. From April 1933 onwards, for example, so-called Aryan paragraphs were added to the legal code, decreeing that Jews could be dismissed without cause, and

barring them from several professions. As the spring leaves began to unfurl in Berlin's parks, the government urged its people to boycott shops and businesses run by Jews. Jewish citizens were no longer permitted to teach at German universities, and before long they were excluded from higher education altogether.

This was why, in late spring 1933, when Kurt Blumenfeld gave Hannah a task, she did not hesitate to throw herself into her work—despite the risks involved. On behalf of the Zionistische Vereinigung für Deutschland, Hannah was charged with finding and compiling anti-Jewish propaganda and statements from various associations, unions, and clubs, in newspapers and other documents. The aim was to alert the media and organizations outside of Germany to the persecution of Jews that had begun. The members of the Zionist organization could not undertake the work themselves—if any one of them was found out, the entire group would be at risk—and so Hannah was the natural choice. "To organize such a collection at that time was to engage in what the Nazis called 'horror propaganda,'" she explained many years later.

Blumenfeld's request came at the exact right moment in Hannah's life, and she threw herself into her work with great enthusiasm. "First of all, it seemed a very intelligent idea to me, and second, it gave me the feeling that something could be done after all," she told Günter Gaus.

Hannah managed to search the archives and skim

newspapers, pamphlets, and leaflets for several weeks before being found out. She was on her way to lunch with her mother one day when she was arrested near Alexanderplatz, a large public square. The police searched her apartment and even interrogated her mother, but Martha was unable to give them any information about what Hannah had been doing. "No, I don't know what she was doing, but whatever she was doing she was right to be doing it, and I would have done the same," she reportedly told the officers.

Hannah was kept in custody for eight days and interrogated for hours on end, but the police failed to get any pertinent information out of her. Their search of her apartment brought up a similar lack of evidence. The officers had seized several notebooks and type-written manuscripts but found nothing incriminating inside; it did not take them long to realize that the manuscripts were simply philosophical works. One notebook containing quotations in an unknown language caused the police some concern, but after several days they established that the text inside was written in Greek, rather than some kind of code.

By this point, Hannah had already realized that she would have to leave Germany, but the arrest was the catalyst that finally spurred her into action. Just days after she was released from custody, she and her mother managed to escape Germany via the dense forests surrounding the Ore Mountains. Hannah and Martha took a train

to Karlsbad (now Karlovy Vary in the Czech Republic) and were invited to dinner by a Sudeten German family whose home straddled the border between Germany and Czechoslovakia. The main entrance to the house was on the German side, the back door on the Czechoslovakian side. Hannah and her mother left Germany via the back door, making their way into the neighbouring country under cover of darkness. That night in 1933 marked the start of Hannah's eighteen years as a stateless person; eighteen years without a citizen's rights or a place to call home.

Five

How Could It Have Happened?

THE POLITICAL DEVELOPMENTS in Germany during the 1930s have been analyzed and discussed by historians, philosophers, and social scientists in countless books and articles. How could so many people, seemingly an entire nation, uncritically accept — or welcome, even — a type of politics directed against a specific group? Laws that excluded people who, until recently, had been friends, neighbours, classmates, and colleagues?

One of the necessary preconditions for the development that led to the Holocaust was the combination of economic depression and the humiliating (in German eyes) settlement following the First World War. Germany was a bitter nation after the Treaty of Versailles; a nation that was tired of suffering and desperate for someone to blame.

"It is an obvious, if frequently forgotten, rule that anti-Jewish feeling acquires political relevance only when it can combine with a major political issue, or when Jewish group interests come into open conflict with those of a major class in society," Hannah Arendt writes in *The Origins of Totalitarianism*. The Jewish people have been forced to play the scapegoat countless times during the history of humanity. Anti-Semitism was not born in 1930s Germany; its roots go back much further than that. The Holocaust was a case of playing on the suspicions and prejudices that already existed within society, and whipping up an anti-Jewish frenzy using anti-Jewish propaganda.

The process that leads to groups and individuals being considered less worthy than others, with fewer rights, does not happen overnight, but once the wheels have been set in motion, things can unfold extremely quickly.

In the book *Humanity: A Moral History of the Twentieth Century*, British philosopher Jonathan Glover provides an answer as to why so many outrages took place during the twentieth century. Glover argues that evil and cruelty flourish in ideologies that have the power to create enemies, robbing the other of their humanity and reducing them to objects. Objectification, according to Glover, is a key part of the strategy: by mocking, heckling, and demeaning the victim, it makes it easier for the perpetrator to carry out their deeds. The purpose of their humiliating actions is to dehumanize the victim, both as

part of the overall denigration process but also in order to psychologically enable the perpetrator to subject the victim to their cruelty.

Philip Zimbardo, an American social psychologist, describes the individual's transition to cruelty in *The Lucifer Effect: Understanding How Good People Turn Evil*. Dehumanization is preceded by depersonalization, which is achieved by depriving victims of identity markers such as clothes or other personal possessions. And yet depersonalization is not just enacted on the victim, depriving the perpetrator of their individual identity is also a clear strategy in war. Like victims, soldiers are stripped of their personal possessions; they are dressed in identical clothing — uniforms — and given identical haircuts, addressed by surname only. Soldiers cease to be individuals, and instead become part of a collective whose sole purpose is to advance the military agenda of the government it serves. Taking away a person's unique sense of being is, therefore, an important element in preparing a person for war.

The preparations Zimbardo describes are necessary to transform "perfectly ordinary" men and women into perpetrators. The reason for this, according to Glover, is that killing or torturing another person is a powerful taboo. One way of circumventing this is to cease to consider the other as human. The enemy — in this case, the Jew — is no longer a person, and therefore no longer in possession of any human worth or rights. Ceasing to be a

person, an individual, in aid of joining the *we*, the collect-
ive, is an equally important precondition to committing
evil. This absorption into the collective creates a sense—
an illusion—of being freed of responsibility.

Central to Glover's argument is the concept of moral
identity. He argues that the majority, possibly even all of
us, have a moral identity that prevents us from commit-
ting evil deeds such as participating in genocide. This
moral identity can, according to Glover, be weakened and
replaced by another kind of moral identity that makes
evil deeds possible; the "Nazi moral identity" is a clear
example of this.

Jonathan Glover's thinking aligns with Hannah
Arendt's arguments in *The Origins of Totalitarianism* and
Eichmann in Jerusalem. In these works, Hannah analyzes
evil, its causes, and why it is able to exist. Both she
and Glover address concepts like indifference and lack
of reflection, rather than phenomena such as cruelty,
sadism, and ill will.

As Hannah would argue, the problem is not the hand-
ful of individuals who choose to do evil. No, the real
problem lies with the people who *fail* to choose, who *fail*
to come to a decision on whether they want to be good
or evil, whether they want to contribute to good or ill.
It was the indifference of the masses and their failure to
take responsibility that made the Holocaust possible, not
just the overt cruelty of a small number of people.

Six

A Special Kind of Evil

THE ANTI-SEMITISM THAT SWEPT across Europe in the 1930s undoubtedly also reared its head on the streets of Paris, where Hannah finally arrived after her escape from Germany at just twenty-six years old. While Martha made her way to Switzerland, Hannah aimed to reconnect with the Zionists she had met through her work in Berlin, who were now living in exile in the French capital. In time, the city would become another impossible place for a Jew to live, but in the years leading up to 1940, it was her home. These years in Paris would prove important to Hannah. If it was in Germany that she got her philosophical education, France was where Hannah learned about politics.

In the fall of 1933, Hannah was one of hundreds of people fleeing the Nazi regime. Some of the refugees were Jews, while others left for their politics. Before long,

they were joined in their relentless search for shelter and work by Jews from Eastern Europe, escaping the growing persecution in their homelands. Many of the refugees lacked papers proving their identities and qualifications, making it extremely difficult for them to find jobs and, ultimately, somewhere to live.

When Hannah arrived in France, the mood was tense. Far from all Parisians welcomed the newcomers with open arms. Over half a million French citizens were out of work, and the competition from the Jewish immigrants was not well received. There was also an acute shortage of housing, particularly in Paris.

Angry Frenchmen began protesting on the streets, with slogans such as *"La France aux français"* (France to the French) soon picked up by the newspapers. Headlines like *"A bas les métèques"* (Down with foreigners) flirted openly with anti-Semitism, and the discrimination began to mount, even within the Jewish diaspora. In her essay "We Refugees," Hannah describes how the French Jews viewed their German brethren with suspicion—the wounds from the First World War had not yet healed—and how the Eastern European Jews thought their German counterparts were not Jewish enough.

Hannah herself was an assimilated Jew. In fact, she was so assimilated that she had not given much thought to her Jewish identity before other people began reminding her that she did, in fact, belong to that group.

Hannah's parents were secular Jews who had never

attached much importance to their Jewish heritage, though they were well aware of the anti-Semitism bubbling just beneath the surface, years before Hitler took power in Germany. Her mother, for example, had encouraged her daughter to report every insult aimed at her in school, and as a result Hannah had learned not to accept being harassed on the basis of her ethnic heritage. She was acutely aware of her Jewishness as a child; she did not look like her tall, blond classmates, as she bluntly put it in her interview with Gaus. She was different. But aside from that, her Jewish identity was not all that important to her. It was other people who insisted on viewing her as a Jew, as The Other, a role that the Jewish people have been forced to play on countless occasions throughout history. The Jews have frequently been portrayed as "they" so that others could be "we."

THE HISTORICAL ORIGINS OF anti-Semitism run deep. As early as late antiquity, myths and prejudices about Jews flourished—for example, that they murdered non-Jews for their blood. Christianity continued to spin the anti-Semitic thread by accusing the Jewish people of having committed deicide by killing Jesus. The incontrovertible fact that both Jesus and his disciples were themselves Jewish has not stopped the Christian institution from cultivating anti-Semitic ideas and hatred. Martin Luther, for example—a central figure

in the Protestant tradition—held views on Jews that were highly dubious, to say the very least. In his 1543 treatise *On the Jews and Their Lies*, Luther describes the Jews as greedy oppressors, accusing them of stealing Christian babies, and he advocates for every last Jew to be driven out of Germany.

There is no doubt that such Christian ideas—not least Luther's—formed a crucial backdrop to the Nazi ideology that cost 6 million Jewish men, women, and children their lives. The cross-pollination of Christianity's hatred of Jews with social Darwinism's concepts of race and the value of different ethnic groups had dire consequences.

In *The Origins of Totalitarianism*, Hannah Arendt argues that anti-Semitism and religion-based Jew-hatred are not the same. She even questions whether anti-Semitism stems from the religious (Christian) hatred of Jews at all, and chooses to separate the two. While anti-Jewish sentiments had been widespread among Europe's educated classes during the nineteenth century, anti-Semitism as an ideology was, she writes, "with very few exceptions, the prerogative of crackpots in general and the lunatic fringe in particular."

So what is the difference? Put simply, anti-Semitism is built on racist notions of an essential "Jewishness" that is defined as bad or inferior. Anti-Semitism harbours macabre theories about Jewish conspiracies and holds the Jewish people responsible for various crimes. Somewhat paradoxically, anti-Semitism considers Jews

to be simultaneously inferior and highly dangerous, and by extension aims to combat, and even eradicate, the Jewish people. One of the theories Hannah defends in *The Origins of Totalitarianism* is that Nazi Germany actually waged two wars: one against the Allies, and another against the Jews.

Religious anti-Jewish sentiments were more *comme il faut*, not least among the educated middle and upper classes, than overtly anti-Semitic ones. In *The Origins of Totalitarianism*, Hannah writes that the Jews were outside the class system — they could not be placed — which created a vacuum for suspicion:

> They did not form a class of their own and they did not belong to any of the classes in their countries. As a group, they were neither workers, middle-class people, landholders, nor peasants. Their wealth seemed to make them part of the middle class, but they did not share in its capitalist development; they were scarcely represented in industrial enterprise and if, in the last stages of their history in Europe, they became employers on a large scale, they employed white-collar personnel and not workers. In other words, although their status was defined through their being Jews, it was not defined through their relationship to another class.

The Jews could not be easily placed, and this created disorder in the hierarchy.

Hannah argued that the Jews have been assigned various roles throughout history — pariah and parvenu, casteless and nouveau riche. The casteless Jew, without financial assets or impressive family ties, is outside all social contexts, exposed and excluded. The successful Jew who has managed to make a fortune, however, is dismissed as a parvenu, a nouveau-riche upstart. Money does not bring such individuals what French sociologist Pierre Bourdieu calls "social capital" — a form of symbolic capital that defines people and groups.

Bourdieu describes this capital in his 1979 work *Distinction: A Social Critique of the Judgement of Taste*. Symbolic capital is categorized into economic, social, and cultural capital. Jews who amassed a fortune possessed economic capital, but they never achieved social capital, which is determined by family ties, networks, and childhood friends. Social capital is like the web between people, one which was inaccessible to the "nouveau riche" Jew.

In *The Origins of Totalitarianism*, Hannah writes that the Jews had to pay a high price for acceptance: "During the 150 years when Jews truly lived amidst, and not just in the neighbourhood of, Western European peoples, they always had to pay with political misery for social glory and with social insult for political success." Any Jew who wanted to become part of a non-Jewish context, she continues, would face the thankless task of being a Jew but not *like* a Jew. It was only then, once a Jew became

estranged from their Jewishness, that the doors of society opened up to them. The price of acceptance was assimilation, and the consequences of assimilation—as we shall see—would prove disastrous.

The text is faded and largely illegible, with only a few lines visible at the top of the page.

Seven

A Lifelong Loyalty

WHEN HANNAH ARRIVED IN PARIS, its rich and vibrant *"année folles"* period was long over. The 1920s had been a creative period in the French capital. The city buzzed with life, and its theatres, concert halls, and nightclubs were full to the brim with men and women determined to have a good time. Legendary venues such as La Cigale, the Olympia, and the Moulin Rouge were thriving. Popular culture in the form of cabarets, languorous chansons, and scantily dressed ballets flourished alongside more highbrow culture, making the city a magnet for artists, writers, and intellectuals who liked to visit its cafés to smoke, drink, and debate for hours.

By 1931, however, the financial crisis—a consequence of the crash on Wall Street a couple of years earlier—had reached Paris. The singing, dancing, and glitter had faded; people had less money to spend, and the birthrate fell. At

around the same time, a wave of immigrants from Russia, Poland, Germany, Italy, Portugal, Spain, and elsewhere in Eastern and Central Europe began to arrive. Political tensions grew, not just in Paris but across the country, and strikes, demonstrations, and clashes between various political groups became everyday occurrences.

By the time Hannah left Germany, she had grown weary of people who were all talk and no action. As she said in an interview many years later: "I left Germany dominated by the idea — of course somewhat exaggerated: Never again! I shall never again get involved in any kind of intellectual business. I want nothing to do with that lot."

Hannah was fortunate and managed to find work as a secretary with Agriculture et Artisanat, an organization that helped to train young émigrés to what was known at the time as Mandatory Palestine. She balanced this with her non-profit role with Youth Aliyah, which had a similar mission protecting and saving Jewish youth from Nazism by sending them to kibbutzim and youth camps in what is now Israel.

Hannah's work for Youth Aliyah was largely practical, involving cooking and making sure the children were properly fed. Many of the Jewish children Youth Aliyah helped to relocate were undernourished and weak, and the organization provided them with food, clothing, and skills training, preparing them for their new lives on a kibbutz. Living in large camps in the countryside,

they learned to grow vegetables and work the land.

Youth Aliyah was founded by Recha Freier, in Berlin, on January 30, 1933, the same day Hitler seized power. The organization managed to send around 5,000 teenagers to Palestine before the outbreak of war. Several thousand more were smuggled out of Germany during the conflict, and following the end of the hostilities, another 15,000 children and teenagers — most of them survivors of concentration camps — were sent to Palestine.

Aside from working for Youth Aliyah, Hannah supported a number of anti-fascist groups in various ways while living a sociable life until war arrived in France. She was part of a large group of Germans in exile — both Jews and non-Jews, artists and writers, activists and intellectuals. Several would become friends for life, and some — who died much too young — would leave a lasting impression on her. Hannah's closest friends included the critical theorist Walter Benjamin; the socialist Erich Cohn-Bendit; the psychoanalyst Fritz Fränkel; the artist Karl Heidenreich; and, of course, Heinrich Blücher, the man who would become Hannah's life partner.

In the spring of 1936, when Hannah first met Blücher — a broad-shouldered, cheerful man with kind eyes — at a lecture in Paris, the carefree years of glamour and decadence had given way to the consequences of the depression. Intellectual life continued to blossom, however, and the lively discussions in Paris's cafés were as intense as ever, a buzz that the wave of immigrants

fleeing political repression and persecution contributed toward. Walter Benjamin, Alexandre Kojève, Jean-Paul Sartre, and Simone de Beauvoir were all enduring stars on the intellectual scene.

Three years had passed since Hannah fled Germany, and she was now aged twenty-nine. On paper, she was still married to Günther Stern, but their relationship had ended years earlier. Hannah was living alone, and she was, in truth, not remotely ready to find love again. Her previous experiences had left her wary.

Heinrich Blücher was, without doubt, a man of action, and his energy and concrete political engagement were part of what attracted Hannah to him; he was different from the men she had known before. Up to that point, Hannah's lovers had all been academics — thin men with soft hands and brooding dispositions: Erwin Loewenson, the essayist; Benno von Wiese, the philosopher; Günther Stern, the promising young philosopher. And, of course, Martin Heidegger, her professor and *Doktorvater* (supervisor).

Love had left its mark on Hannah. After her relationship with Martin and the fizzling-out of her marriage to Günther, she was cautious by nature. She had, as she told her friend Anne Mendelsohn Weil, made a promise to herself never to love another man. Love, or perhaps blind passion, terrified her.

Heinrich was often laughing, and he made Hannah laugh, too — something she had not often experienced

during her student days as Martin's lover, nor in her brief marriage to Günther.

Born and raised in Berlin, Heinrich came from the German working class, and was to all intents and purposes an autodidact. He had a huge thirst for knowledge, but only a minor interest in formal education. He spent what little money he had on books, and he avoided work whenever possible in order to read. When Hannah and Heinrich first met, Hannah was deeply involved in her work with the Zionist movement. Oddly enough, despite not being a Jew, Heinrich had a history with Zionism—he had been a member of a Zionist youth group as a young man.

Like Hannah, cheerful, sociable Heinrich was married when they first met. He too was a refugee, but as a result of his political engagement in the Spartacus League—a revolutionary Marxist movement founded by Rosa Luxemburg (someone Hannah would go on to write about) among others, and active in Germany between 1916 and 1919. After 1919, the League joined with other groups to form Germany's Communist Party.

Heinrich's activist spirit and political engagement had awoken early, and powerfully. He had, however, quickly abandoned Zionism in favour of Marxism. As a teen, he read Marx, Engels, and Trotsky, and went to various lectures on military history.

While Hannah was reading Kierkegaard and Kant at school in Königsberg, Heinrich had been fighting on the

streets of Berlin alongside the other Spartacus League members in their 1919 uprising. Working with author and composer Robert Gilbert during the 1920s — Berlin's most decadent period — Heinrich had been both a political writer and created a number of operettas, musicals, and films.

For Heinrich, like Hannah, the escape from Berlin had been a hasty affair. He had not managed to take anything with him and had no identity documents, but he received financial support from his friend Lotte Sempell, who also provided him with a place to stay from time to time. Lotte, the daughter of a wealthy industrialist from Westphalia, viewed her support of Heinrich and the other political refugees from Germany as a form of protest against Hitler. In exchange, through conversations and discussions with Heinrich and his friends, she received a comprehensive political education.

A few weeks after their first meeting, Hannah invited Heinrich over for dinner. He arrived in costume as his alter ego, Heinrich Larsen, a tourist from the German bourgeoisie — almost his own class enemy, you might say — wearing a suit and hat, carrying a cane. Hannah gave him the title "Monsieur" — a nickname that stuck for life.

Chanan Klenbort, a Jewish author who had fled Poland, was also invited, as a chaperone. It was a beautiful June evening, and the conversation flowed between Hannah and Heinrich. Chanan made several attempts to

leave, but was talked into staying a while longer every time. It wasn't until two in the morning that the dinner party finally ended, seemingly a complete success.

One month later, in July 1936, the Spanish Civil War broke out between the Republicans (the left and the bourgeois centre) and the Nationalists (the right and the military) led by Franco. The Nazi regime, however, was still doing its best to put on a good front during the bright European summer. Berlin hosted the Olympic Games, and cheerful visitors filled the city's streets— though German competitors of Jewish or Roma origin were barred.

Chanan Klenbort travelled to Spain to cover the war for a Polish newspaper, and when he returned to Paris, he invited Hannah over for dinner. But it was Heinrich who opened the door; he had in fact moved in with Chanan during the summer.

HANNAH AND HEINRICH'S LOVE for each other was obvious from the very outset. Theirs was a relationship of equals, between two grown adults who had chosen each other. Hannah was not his muse, the way she had been with previous lovers; she and Heinrich completed each other. A sense of mutual respect existed between them, an appreciation of their different experiences and knowledge. There was an immediate sense of trust between Hannah and Heinrich that she had never encountered

before — not with Martin, the man she had worshipped for many years, nor even with the man she had married, Günther.

In a letter sent to Heinrich from Geneva on September 18, 1937, Hannah wrote:

> And when I met you, suddenly I was no longer afraid — after that first fright, which was just a childish fright pretending to be grown up. It still seems incredible to me that I managed to get both things, the "love of my life" and a oneness with my self. And yet, I only got the one thing when I got the other. But finally I also know what happiness is.

Heinrich replied in a letter sent from Paris on September 19:

> And then a letter from you arrives, making me crazy with joy. I've shown you what happiness is? I make you happy as you make me happy? After all, you are my happiness, so did I show you to yourself? You turned into who you are? I did too. I turned you, my little darling, from a girl into a woman? How marvelous — but how did I manage that, because it was only through you that I really became a man.

In her love for Heinrich, Hannah felt safe. It made her happy, free, and full of self-confidence. They brought out the best in each other, and isn't that precisely what

love should do? Love is not the constant rollercoaster, the emotional whirlwind, or the desperation described in *The Sorrows of Young Werther* or *The Magic Mountain*.

Yet that does not mean that the love Hannah and Heinrich shared was lukewarm or feeble. On the contrary, it is this type of love — a comforting, reliable, strong love — that can be groundbreaking, can transform a person and their life. In *The Human Condition*, Hannah writes that "love, by its very nature, is unworldly" and "antipolitical," going on to say that "love, by reason of its passion, destroys the in-between which relates us to and separates us from others." Hannah believed, in other words, that love causes the distance between two people to disappear.

In her relationship with Heinrich, Hannah developed her own views around love and fidelity — closer to a philosophy, in truth — that were far removed from the conventional, romantic vision she had previously held. This development was neither painless nor easy for Hannah. Heinrich was indeed older, with far more experience, and with notions of love that were shaped by the anarchistic currents of the time. He gave Hannah both security and freedom, but demanded the same from her. Hannah's romantic idea of being everything to one's lover — borrowed from poetry and literature — received a few knocks during the course of their long relationship, but the independence they granted each other also grew, as did their trust and friendship.

Eight

La drôle de guerre

IN THE SUMMER OF 1936, just a few months after Hannah met Heinrich, she travelled to Geneva to take part in the founding of the Jewish World Congress. Newly in love, she wrote to Heinrich every day, and he replied by return mail. Aside from declarations of love, their letters are full of anxiety about the situation in Europe. Hannah's frustration over the fact that the escalating persecution of Jews was not being taken seriously—even by Jews themselves—is a recurring theme. On August 8, for example, she wrote:

> At the press conference yesterday, and also in some of the press releases, there's talk of all kinds of oppressive political measures, both economic and legal. But not a word about our being pogromized in Poland! Who will speak up if we don't? To make up for that,

the representative of the Polish government will make an official appearance at the League of Nations tonight! The Polish Jews will stop our mouths just as the German Jews did three years ago. And in the end we'll all go to hell.

There is no mistaking Hannah's sense of powerlessness here. She could not understand why her friends in the World Zionist Organization seemed to want to gloss over what was happening, as though they were ashamed or possibly even afraid that the persecution would worsen if they pushed back.

This was neither the first nor the last time Hannah would come close to despair over the fact that those around her did not seem to understand what was going on. From its very early stages, she had been aware of the dangers of the process that had begun in Germany with a sharpening of restrictions on Jewish freedoms, and with discrimination, exclusion, and persecution. When she chose to leave her homeland, many were still living under the delusional belief that things would work out, that life would get better—but, as we now know, that was not to be. Things got much worse.

In 1937, there were around 15,000 German refugees in Paris, and when Hitler annexed Austria on March 13, 1938, a new wave of Jewish refugees arrived. Hannah's mother, Martha, soon followed, finally arriving in France after having spent the time since her escape from Berlin

living with a friend in Switzerland. By 1939, it was time to reunite with her daughter in Paris.

Early that summer, Hannah and Heinrich moved to a new, slightly less cramped apartment on rue de la Convention, making space for Martha. Just four months after Martha arrived in Paris, war broke out.

"We were very poor, we were hunted down, we had to flee, by hook or by crook we somehow had to get through," Hannah later said about her years in Paris. "But we were young. I even had a little fun with it—I can't deny it."

Hannah and Heinrich were part of a large group of intellectuals who met in bars and cafés or at one another's apartments—often at Walter Benjamin's apartment on rue Dombasle. Walter, or Benji, as Hannah affectionately called him, was—like Heinrich—born and raised in Berlin. He was an art and literary critic, and he had formulated an eclectic, headstrong philosophy, taking elements from Marxism and Jewish mysticism. In 1933, his books were burned by the Nazis, but he had already fled Germany by that point—he had escaped with Hannah's first husband, Günther Stern, who also happened to be his cousin, in 1932.

Like Hannah, Walter was interested in Zionism, and his closest friend, the mystic Gershom Scholem, would eventually become one of Hannah's good friends. Walter's journey into exile had begun in Ibiza and Nice before turning to Denmark, where he spent some time living with Bertolt Brecht.

Walter eventually settled in Paris, where he, Hannah, and Heinrich grew very close. Hannah took on an almost motherly role in relation to Walter. He seems to have been the type of man—sickly, easily confused, fumbling, and helpless—who woke nurturing instincts in people. He was also a beautiful man, with a sensual mouth and pained eyes.

ON SEPTEMBER 3, 1939, Hannah was on vacation with Heinrich and Walter when news of the outbreak of war reached them. They had rented a house in a small village outside of Paris in order to read, write, and talk, and their days were spent smoking, drinking coffee, working, and conversing; they were enjoying the late summer and the period of calm. Heinrich had been reading Kant, Walter had managed to finish a long essay on Baudelaire, and Hannah had been working on a text about the roots of anti-Semitism. In the evenings, embraced by warm darkness, they drank wine, discussed political issues, and thought about the future.

The headlines that reached them that morning marked the beginning of the period called the *"Sitzkrieg,"* *"la drôle de guerre,"* or the Phony War as it is known in English. France and Great Britain had given Germany an ultimatum to withdraw its troops from Poland, and at eleven o'clock that same day, after the Germans defied their demands, they declared war. What followed was a

strange period in which the countries were formally at war, but failed to take any real military action; the great powers simply sat and waited, watching one another. This would, however, come to an abrupt end less than a year later, in spring, as German troops marched into France.

With the declaration of war in 1939, the relative calm the three friends had managed to create in their rented house in the country was shattered. Violence and chaos were now on their doorstep. The conflict they had long feared was approaching, and the troubled outside world had reached the small, peaceful village in which Hannah, Heinrich, and Walter had sought refuge. How does a person react when forced to face evil? She can run, she can fight; she can be struck down by fear, gripped by panic, struggle on—or she can give up.

Hannah and Heinrich remained composed when they heard the news, but Walter began to panic. He was afraid that Paris would be bombed, and he decided to end his vacation and head further north, to Meaux. This would prove a fateful decision, because Meaux was home to a military base that the Germans had in their sights. No bombs fell on Paris that autumn, but Meaux was subjected to assault from the air. Walter hurried back to the capital, which—so far—had been spared the Germans' bombs.

Hannah warmly recalls this episode in *Men in Dark Times*, describing it as typically Walter: in his attempt to

escape German aggression, he had managed to flee to the only place in France that was actually bombed during the fall of 1939. She describes Walter as a man whose life—and, as it would turn out, death—was characterized by bad luck and an unfortunate knack for being in the wrong place at the wrong time.

In an essay on Marcel Proust, Walter Benjamin cites Jacques Rivière's description of the great author: "Marcel Proust died of the same inexperience as enabled him to write his work. He died of unworldliness and because he lacked the understanding to alter living conditions that had begun to crush him. He died because he did not know how to light a fire or open a window." Hannah, too, refers to this quotation, arguing that, in citing Rivière, Walter was, in fact, describing himself. Like Proust, Walter was completely unable to change the circumstances of his life—even when those circumstances threatened to overcome him.

After just a few days of being back in Paris, Hannah and Heinrich were faced with yet another repercussion of war. Like all other foreign men with a "suspect political past," Heinrich was instructed to report to an internment camp. Walter managed to escape a similar fate, thanks largely to his weak physical health and the efforts of diplomat and poet Saint-John Perse.

Heinrich was interned in Villemalard along with his friends Peter Huber and Erich Cohn-Bendit. The men spent their days working outside in the cold and the

rain, and their nights sleeping on mattresses filled with mouldy straw in a drafty barn. It was a diverse group of men who were forced to coexist under less-than-pleasant circumstances — some, like Heinrich and Peter, were communists; others were Orthodox Jews; and one man was a former officer in the German Wehrmacht.

DURING THE MONTHS HEINRICH was interned in the camp, he and Hannah corresponded back and forth between Villemalard and Paris. The internees were permitted to write letters on Saturdays and Tuesdays, and they were also allowed to receive parcels. In one of the first letters from Heinrich to Hannah, he asked for "red wine, cigarettes, and chocolate," but as the weather worsened, he asked her to send:

1. My ski boots
2. My winter jacket
3. Pants (Manchester velvet, beige or brown)
4. My winter socks
5. 2 shirts
6. A stainless steel kitchen knife (not a pointed one!)
7. Mess tin
8. [. . .] to wash my head
9. My small pipe (the one you gave me as a present)
10. My tobacco pouch

Heinrich received a large parcel just eleven days after sending his list to Hannah, and wrote, "you see, communications are perfect now." In one of his last letters from Villemalard, dated November 28, 1939, the tone is less cheerful. Heinrich was suffering from kidney stones, and had just spent his eighth day in a row ill. "I find my fundamental opinions concerning the European situation have gotten even stronger," he wrote to Hannah from his sickbed. "As Napoleon predicted on St. Helena, Europe is faced with the option of whether it wants to be ruled by Cossacks or by Republicans." Russia or America, that was the question. Who would seize power? Who would Europe be forced to obey?

When Napoleon posed his question, Europe was a patchwork of minor states and kingdoms. They were sophisticated, with complex cultures, but they were also small, and this—according to Napoleon—made them vulnerable: there were too few of them to be able to withstand the raw, crude Cossacks and the vulgar, uneducated Americans, both with vast populations. What Russia and the United States lacked in finesse, they made up for in strength. "The Children of Hercules," as Napoleon called the two nations, would take their revenge on Europe— and one of these despised children would, he predicted, conquer Europe.

Napoleon's query, or fear—like Heinrich's—now seems prophetic: communism or capitalism? The question portends the Cold War, which lasted for decades.

But the Third Reich came before all that. Heinrich likely suspected as much from his sickbed—Germany and France were at war, after all—yet it seems unlikely that he could have imagined the extent of what was to come.

When Heinrich was finally released from the labour camp and its drafty barn, he was emaciated and still suffering from kidney stones. Yet just a few days after his return to Paris, he and Hannah got married.

The ceremony was a simple one, at the city hall, but Hannah and Heinrich's decision to marry would prove crucial going forward. The emergency visas later given out by the United States were awarded exclusively to single women and married couples, and in the chaos that soon descended over the country, once the Phony War ended and bombs began to fall across the north of France, marriage ceremonies were hardly the first priority for authorities.

For several months, life returned almost to normal for Hannah and Heinrich. They celebrated Heinrich's forty-first birthday, and they continued to read, write, and work. Together with Walter, they began taking English lessons. Hannah was convinced they should be preparing themselves for a life in the U.S. True to her nature, she anticipated the worst: that they would have to flee Europe in order to save their lives.

Both Heinrich and Walter thought English an appalling language. Indeed, Walter liked to joke that he needed only learn enough English to be able to say that he

detested it, claiming, in his typically macabre way, that he would rather live a short life in France than a long life in the United States. Neither Walter nor Heinrich seemed to be taking things seriously. The prospect of being forced to leave France, of having to flee once again, escaping Europe for America, still seemed a distant possibility. But with the announcement of a new order declaring that all German citizens in France, men and women alike, must be interned, everything changed.

Nine

Camp Gurs

THE DETENTION ORDER was published in all French newspapers on May 5, 1940. The brief announcement from the governor general of Paris that Hannah and Heinrich read in *Le Temps* urged all men and all childless women between the ages of seventeen and fifty-five, from Germany, the Saar region on the border of France and Germany, and Danzig (now Gdańsk), to report for "transport" to internment camps; they were now considered "enemy aliens" in France. Hannah and her husband both shared the status of refugee. Heinrich may not have been Jewish, but he was a dissident and a communist.

The announcement in the newspaper was unambiguous: the men were to make their way to the Stade Buffalo, a sports complex on the outskirts of Paris, on May 14, and the women to the Vélodrome d'Hiver on May 15. Ten days—that was how long Hannah had to prepare. Nine

days with the man she loved. When Heinrich left their apartment in Paris on May 14, he had no idea where he would be sent. The couple couldn't be sure they would ever see each other again.

According to the internment order, every "enemy alien" was permitted to take enough food for two days, plus a mug, a plate, and cutlery, as well as a bag or rucksack weighing a maximum of thirty kilos.

On May 15, Hannah made her way to the Vélodrome d'Hiver, an enormous indoor cycling track, with her bag. For the next eight days, she and around 2,300 other women were locked beneath the velodrome's great glass roof. Their time there was stuffy and uneventful; no one knew what was going to happen, and no one told the internees anything. Whenever a plane flew overhead, the women feared it was a German bomber, ready to attack. Hannah pictured the roof shattering into millions of pieces—some kind of Parisian *Kristallnacht*, a torrential shower of glass pouring down over the women being held prisoner inside. In order to reassure one another, the women reminded themselves how grateful they were that the guards were Frenchmen and not SS troops. They told themselves they were beyond the enemy's reach, and tried to avoid reflecting on the fact that they had been locked up by people who had once claimed to be their friends.

In addition to the handful of belongings Hannah packed, she took the same poem that had helped her

husband during his time in Villemalard. The poem, by Bertolt Brecht, was unpublished at the time, but Heinrich had memorized it. As he later explained to Hannah, it helped him determine who was a friend and who was not; either they understood it, or they didn't:

> He learnt how quite soft water, by attrition
> Over the years will grind strong rocks away.
> In other words, that hardness must lose the day.

Like Heinrich, Brecht was a dissident, a political refugee. He had been one of Germany's most lauded cultural figures during the 1920s, winning prestigious awards and seeing his plays performed on the biggest stages. In 1926, however, he began to study Marx, and later he wrote several works influenced by Marxism.

Shortly after Hitler seized power in 1933, Brecht left Germany to take refuge with the Danish author Karin Michaëlis, and when he eventually bought his own property there, in Svendborg on the island of Funen, Walter Benjamin paid him a visit. A series of black-and-white photographs show the two friends playing chess beneath a pear tree in Brecht's garden, both deeply focused on the game. Brecht, facing the camera, is squinting slightly in the sun. He has a fat cigar in one hand, and he looks relaxed. A smile plays on his lips as he studies Walter, who is hunched over and frowning, thinking about his next move. The chessboard is laid out on a simple wooden

table, and the two men are sitting on rickety wooden chairs, surrounded by a lush garden of berry bushes and fruit trees. There are hollyhocks growing by the white half-timbered house in the background.

Aside from that visit in the summer of 1934, when the photo was most likely taken, Walter paid his friend another two visits, in 1936 and 1938. From the black-and-white images, it is difficult to see what could be so dangerous or despicable about the two men—which is how they were viewed by the authorities in their homeland, where the Nazi regime burned their books. The poem that Heinrich found so comforting was eventually published in the collection *Svendborger Gedichte* (*Svendborg Poems*), now considered one of the most important works of German exile literature.

ON MAY 23, HANNAH and the other women were finally taken from the Vélodrome d'Hiver and loaded into a caravan of buses that drove along the banks of the Seine, past the Louvre. Several of the women on board began to cry. They knew it could be the last time they ever saw Paris, the city that had, for some of them, been their home for years. Hannah did not cry. After almost seven years in Paris, she considered the city hers, and she told herself she would return to her life there, and to Heinrich.

The buses pulled up outside the Gare de Lyon, and from there the women were put onto a train to Gurs,

where a large internment camp awaited them. The 2,364 women from Paris were interned alongside groups of men and women from elsewhere in France. By the end of June that year, there were 6,536 internees in Camp Gurs, which was originally built to house political refugees from Spain—Republicans who had fought Franco's army and were forced to flee after the end of the civil war in 1939. When Hannah arrived, only one block of the camp—eight barracks in total—was housing Spaniards. The vast majority of the men and women in the camp were German Jews who had been forced to leave the country in which they had been born and raised, a country that had suddenly begun to view them as something other than what they considered themselves to be: Germans.

The camp was built following the same principle as an ancient Roman city. One road, a *cardo*, split the camp in two lengthwise, and another larger road, a *decumanus*, split it crosswise. Eight further roads divided the camp into blocks. The whole thing was surrounded by barbed wire and illuminated by floodlights.

Camp Gurs was situated at the foot of the Pyrenees, which had an impact on the climate of the area. Hannah describes how the air quivered with heat during the day, only to be replaced by thunderstorms and torrential downpours at night. The constant nightly rain transformed the roads in the camp to mud, leaving the internees' clothes damp and smelling like washrags.

Since only one of the barracks had running water, it was difficult to maintain personal hygiene, but Hannah made sure to wash every day, to comb her short, curly hair, and to keep her clothing as clean as possible.

Kaethe Hirsch, whose diaries from Gurs were later published, wrote that the worst part about the camp was the boredom. It must have been incredibly tempting simply to sit around, feeling sorry for oneself. Yet Hannah refused to fall victim to that temptation, encouraging the other women to keep themselves neat and tidy — well aware of the need to preserve morale, not to let herself go downhill either physically or mentally.

THE TIME HANNAH SPENT in the camp was as regimented as the camp itself. Wake up, wash, clean the barracks, empty the latrines. There was little variety in the food, and the internees were typically served dried, salted fish. There was no allowance for individual choice. No physical violence seems to have taken place at Gurs, but the psychological violence was marked, the wielding of power absolute. The prisoners in the camp were no longer free, and had been denied all power over their lives. Someone else was in charge, someone who used their power to make the internees do whatever he or she wanted. Is that not simply another form of violence?

In her discussion of violence as a phenomenon in *On Violence*, Hannah takes as her starting point the American

sociologist Charles Wright Mills's claim that "the ultimate kind of power is violence." There is, Hannah argues, widespread agreement among political theorists on both the left and the right that violence is nothing more than "the most flagrant manifestation of power," yet Hannah herself does not immediately accept that definition — she rarely made things that easy for herself. Instead, she argues, we must first agree on what we mean by "power."

Power, wrote Voltaire, "consists in making others act as I choose." Max Weber's definition echoes this. In Weber's opinion, power is present every time we assert our will "against the resistance" of others. Meanwhile, the French philosopher Bertrand de Jouvenel writes: "To command and to be obeyed: without that, there is no power — with it no other attribute is needed for it to be ... The thing without which it cannot be: that essence is command."

Hannah argues that phenomena such as strength, authority, power, and violence are related, but by no means synonymous:

> Politically speaking, it is insufficient to say that power and violence are not the same. Power and violence are opposites; where the one rules absolutely, the other is absent. Violence appears where power is in jeopardy, but left to its own course it ends in power's disappearance. This implies that it is not correct to think of the opposite of violence as non-violence; to speak of

non-violent power is actually redundant. Violence can destroy power; it is utterly incapable of creating it.

When there is no power, Hannah concluded, violence reigns supreme.

FRANCE CAPITULATED ON JUNE 22, 1940. Marshal Philippe Pétain, who replaced Prime Minister Paul Reynard, announced the decision over the radio. The government had left Paris on June 10, and the British had abandoned Dunkirk, Calais, and western France back in late May. Rumours of the country's surrender to Germany spread like wildfire among the women in Camp Gurs, and anxiety levels quickly rose. No one—neither Hannah's fellow inmates nor the guards—knew what would happen next. What would capitulation mean for the German citizens being held behind the barbed-wire fences? Would the prisoners be handed over to the occupying forces? Would they be freed? Speculation was rife, and fear and resignation mixed with hope and despair.

Hannah realized that an opportunity to leave the camp, to flee, would soon present itself. The chain of power was broken, and disorder and violence awaited them. In the confusion and chaos that arose, a window appeared, and it was imperative to act quickly. Sooner or later, she knew, the Nazis would take over the camp, and the likelihood that they would free the Jews being held

there was next to none. Yet again, the instinct to assume the worst guided her through.

In the end, it proved easier to leave the camp than Hannah could ever have imagined. The day after France's capitulation, the prisoners being held in Gurs were given the option to leave. The guards handed them release papers and strict orders to leave the department of Pyrénées-Atlantiques within twenty-four hours. They were told that there was no functioning public transport, neither buses nor trains, that they would have to travel on foot, and that they should take as little as possible with them. Anyone still within the region after twenty-four hours would, the guards told them, be interned again.

For Hannah, the decision was an easy one. She packed lightly and tried to make the other women understand that they too should seize the opportunity to leave. Despite this, to Hannah's great despair, many of the imprisoned women chose to stay; they preferred the relative safety of the camp to the uncertain freedom of the outside world. In 1962, Hannah wrote an article about the women who chose to stay behind for *Midstream* magazine: "None of us could 'describe' what lay in store for those who remained behind. All we could do was to tell them what we expected would happen—the camp would be handed over to the victorious Germans. (About 200 women of a total of 7,000 left.)"

Hannah's fears proved true, and Camp Gurs was indeed taken over by the Germans. In the fall of 1940,

just a few months after Hannah left the camp, another
6,000 internees arrived at Gurs—Jews from Baden and
Saar-Pfalz who had been transported into France by
Adolf Eichmann with the co-operation of France's new
collaborationist Vichy regime. As the number of prison-
ers grew, conditions in the camp worsened. Many people
died, from both malnutrition and illness, and those who
survived were ultimately sent to concentration camps in
Germany over the course of 1942 and 1943.

Hannah herself left Gurs as quickly as she could, join-
ing the steady stream of people who had been released
from other camps. The roads were full of those who had
left the occupied areas of France—thousands of men and
women on the move, all fleeing something, few with any
real destination in mind. They slept in barns or on hay
bales beneath the night sky, occasionally meeting farmers
who took pity on them and provided them with room
and board in exchange for temporary work.

Arthur Koestler, whose book *Scum of the Earth* docu-
ments his own experiences of being interned at Le Vernet,
wrote about the women from Gurs:

> Saw several German émigré women previously interned
> in concentration camp at Gurs—now released, don't
> know where to go, what to do. Talked to one in a café;
> said she is sending telegrams to all concentration camps
> in non-occupied France, trying to find her husband;
> praying that he should not be in occupied territory.

Hundreds of women in her case living in Castelnau, Navarrenx, Sus, Geronce and other villages round about. Population calls them *les Gursiennes*. Peasants lend rooms to them or let them work in the fields *au pair*. They look undernourished, exhausted, but tidy. All wear turbans *à la mode*, coloured handkerchiefs round the head.

Perhaps the women from Gurs wore colourful turbans because it was so difficult to wash their hair in the camp, or maybe it was to protect their hair. Perhaps Hannah, too, wore a turban over her short, dark hair as she walked away from Gurs, away from Pyrénées-Atlantiques.

On leaving the camp, Hannah had no idea where Heinrich was, but, like the woman Koestler describes in his book, she attempted to find her husband. As per the national order, Heinrich had reported to the Stade Buffalo cycling track for onward transport on May 14, but his final destination had remained a mystery. Since their kiss farewell that morning in May, they had not had any contact at all.

Ten

Montauban

RETURNING TO THE APARTMENT in Paris, which was now under German occupation, was not an option, so Hannah set her sights on the free zone instead. She walked along the edge of the Pyrenees, toward the Mediterranean, arriving by chance in Lourdes. The small town, which welcomes hundreds of thousands of pilgrims every year, occupies a pretty spot at the foot of the mountains. A river runs through its centre, and just outside of town is the cave where, according to legend, the Virgin Mary appeared to a young girl called Bernadette.

To her great joy, Hannah found Walter Benjamin in Lourdes. He had realized he would be forced to leave the capital after the Gestapo searched his apartment, and had managed to get onto the last train departing Paris. The very thought of their hostile hands on his belongings had made Walter uncomfortable at home, and the Gestapo

had also seized many of the texts he was working on, destroying a number of his books.

Hannah, exhausted and aching after several days of walking, with blisters on her feet, rested up with Walter. He was grateful for the company, and he took care of her in his typically fumbling way. Hannah describes her time in Lourdes in a letter to her good friend Gershom Scholem:

This was the time of defeat, and after a few days the trains stopped running. No one knew what had happened to families, husbands, children, and friends. Benji and I played chess from morning to evening, and between games we read newspapers, to the extent we could get our hands on them. Everything was as fine as could be — until the ceasefire terms were published, along with the famous extradition clause. But even then I can't say that Benjamin fell into a full-blown panic, even if we were both feeling anxious. Mind you, when news reached us of the first suicide among those in internment fleeing from the Germans, Benjamin began for the first time to talk repeatedly to me about suicide: there was always "that" way out.

Hannah became increasingly concerned by her good friend's attitude, and she insisted that such an act — committing suicide — would be playing into the Nazis' hands. That was precisely what they wanted, for Jews to die — so why give them the satisfaction?

After a few weeks in Lourdes with Walter, Hannah set off again. Her destination was Montauban, a small town in the south of France that had become something of a sanctuary for refugees.

The mayor, Fernand Balès, was a staunch socialist who refused point-blank to obey the Vichy regime. Balès permitted refugees to move into the properties that had been abandoned in the general confusion that arose after France's capitulation, and thousands of people—refugees who had managed to leave their detention camps before it was too late—descended on Montauban. They had been robbed of everything, and every one of them was searching for someone.

The small medieval town was bathed in soft pink light when Hannah arrived on foot after several days of walking. Montauban's low buildings are tiled in various shades of red, from the palest of pinks to the deepest terracotta, and the narrow streets are paved. A river flows through the centre, and under different circumstances, Hannah would have no doubt noted how beautiful it was. But in the summer of 1940, her thoughts were elsewhere. Her entire being was focused on finding Heinrich again.

Hannah did not stay in the picturesque little town for long. She knew that her friend, Lotte Klenbort, had rented a small house just outside of Montauban in order to get away from Paris, and her plan was to stay there. She was hoping that Heinrich had been thinking along similar lines, and that he too was making his way to Montauban.

Unlike when he was interned in Villemalard, they had been unable to write to each other, and neither knew where the other had ended up. Wherever Hannah turned, she met people searching for their children, parents, and loved ones. They showed one another photographs, hoping to bump into someone with information about whoever they were looking for—perhaps they had been in the same camp, or maybe they had met on the road? The walls of Montauban's cafés were plastered with handwritten notes full of descriptions and contact details.

From Lotte's house, Hannah cycled into Montauban several times a week in order to keep up to date with developments in the war, but above all to search for information about Heinrich. Then, one day, after weeks of hope and despair, there he was—standing right in front of her on a street in Montauban.

If this were a novel, it would be difficult to make readers believe such a happy, unlikely coincidence: the heroine of our story, alone and afraid in a country of 40 million people, recently released from an internment camp, suddenly finds herself face-to-face with the man she loves—someone who, like her, had been suffering in a prison camp for months.

However unlikely it seems, that was precisely what happened. Despite everything, Hannah and Heinrich found each other again. They fell into each other's arms, right there in the middle of Montauban's biggest, busiest street, and it was some time before they let each other go.

The camp where Heinrich was interned had been evacuated when the Germans reached Paris. The guards had ordered the internees to march south, where they would be admitted to another camp, but as German planes swept overhead, shooting down at the line of prisoners, the guards decided to let them flee. Heinrich had continued to make his way south, away from Paris, toward the free zone—joining the thousands of bikes, cars, and people migrating away from German-controlled territory just like Hannah had.

Hannah and Heinrich spent a short time with Lotte in her rented house, but they soon managed to find a small apartment of their own in Montauban. It quickly became a meeting place, and the couple almost managed to recreate the social life they had once enjoyed in Paris. The Weil sisters, the Cohn-Bendits, the Klenbort family, Peter Huber, and Walter Benjamin all paid visits to their small flat above a photography studio, and the neurologist Fritz Fränkel also stopped by on his way overseas.

It was a hot, dry summer, and discussions about the political situation and what the future might hold were endless. What was going to happen? To France, to Europe? To the Jewish people? Should they stay and hope for the best, or was it time to leave? If so, where should they go, and how? Fritz Fränkel had left for Mexico, Walter Benjamin had reluctantly accepted the prospect of leaving Europe for America, and by 1940, Bertolt Brecht was living in Sweden after several years in Denmark.

Step by step, the Vichy regime was moving in an increasingly anti-Semitic direction. Hannah recognized the process from what had taken place in Germany, and she knew how it would end. It began gradually, but would ultimately culminate in exclusion and internment. A committee was set up that summer to review the citizenship of the 500,000 people of all nationalities who had become naturalized French citizens since 1927. It was a case of identifying Jews: identifying and excluding them.

Hannah and Heinrich tried to distract themselves and pass the time by reading, but time rarely moves as slowly — and so cruelly fast — as it does when we are faced with uncertainty. Everything seems to stand still while also hurtling forward. In an essay on Walter Benjamin, Hannah would later describe that summer as "the darkest moment of the war." France had fallen, England was under threat, and the Hitler–Stalin pact was still intact, meaning close collaboration between the two most powerful intelligence services in Europe.

While Heinrich continued to study Kant, Hannah read Marcel Proust, Carl von Clausewitz, and Georges Simenon — works that would leave their mark on *The Origins of Totalitarianism*. Simenon's depiction of the French police proved particularly valuable to Hannah, especially on a personal level.

In October 1940, all Jews in France were ordered to report to the nearest police station — an unabashed call

for registration. Hannah immediately refused. There was no way she would voluntarily turn herself over to the authorities. Some of her friends thought she was being conspiratorial when she forbade them from obeying the order. Several of them likely laughed as she claimed that the French police could not be trusted, referring to one of Simenon's crime novels as proof. The French police would never behave like that!

The fact that Hannah and Heinrich, as well as the majority of their friends, refused to register meant that, in addition to being stateless, they were now also considered illegal. Those who had obeyed the order to register with the French police, however, providing the addresses at which they were staying, were later arrested and handed over to the Germans.

It had become high time to leave France.

Eleven

The Meaning of Hope:
On Suicide

IT WASN'T UNTIL MUCH LATER, years after she escaped
the camp and left Europe, that Hannah confessed to
Kurt Blumenfeld, her friend from Berlin, that she had
considered taking her own life while she was locked up
at Gurs. The mud, the rats, the constant hunger, and the
cramped, dark barracks; the pungent smell of the other
women's bodies...it was all incredibly trying, and yet
that was not the reason she began thinking about suicide.
No, it was something else, something greater and much
more difficult: an overwhelming sense that the world
was beyond saving.

What does a person do if she loses all hope? She gives
up. The ability to imagine a future, a situation beyond
the present, is vital to the survival of humankind. Only
those who retain that ability — that hope — can survive

evil and inhumanity. In 1943, after Hannah had reached safety in the United States, she wrote about the relationship between faith, hope, and survival in her essay "We Refugees," commissioned by the Jewish magazine the *Menorah Journal*. Europe's Jews were not the first to be persecuted, Hannah wrote, but "we are the first non-religious Jews persecuted—and we are the first ones who, not only *in extremis*, answer with suicide." To those with no faith, there is no obstacle to suicide, no god to forbid it, no hell in which to burn for all eternity.

When I read about the despair Hannah felt in Gurs, I found myself thinking about Viktor Frankl, the Austrian neurologist and psychiatrist, and his arguments around meaning and hope. "He who has a *why* to live for can bear with almost any *how*," he writes in *Man's Search for Meaning*, paraphrasing Nietzsche. Frankl's insight was deeply personal. He was sent to the Theresienstadt ghetto in 1942, and while he managed to survive four different concentration camps, he lost his wife and his parents. Reflecting on how he managed to survive, he attaches great importance to his ability to feel both hope and meaning: if someone has a why, they can endure almost anything. "Life is never made unbearable by circumstances, but only by lack of meaning and purpose," he writes.

Meaning and purpose: this is precisely what religion can provide; a belief in the transcendental, something beyond this life—a deity who has a plan, who will

protect you. Hannah lacked this faith. She grew up in a home that harboured little interest in religious matters. Her parents believed in socialism, not God; Martha and Paul were social democrats. Hannah's grandparents, however, were believers, and she had often accompanied them to synagogue.

As a teenager in Königsberg, Hannah went on to read Kant, Jaspers, and Kierkegaard, and it isn't hard to see the deep impact their writing had on her thinking, the way ideas that make an impression on us during our youth often do. Taken together, the three thinkers make an interesting foundation on which to build a philosophy, an attitude toward life—maybe even a system: Kant, with his unerring faith in humankind's reason and good will, and in categorical imperatives; Jaspers, with his notions of limit situations; and Kierkegaard, whose romantic existentialism emphasizes bravery and the irrational rather than reason, so fundamental to Kant's philosophical system.

Being confronted with human mortality—our own, and others'—is the background against which we must live our lives, and in the situation in which Hannah found herself in 1940, interned in a camp for "undesirables," death must have felt utterly tangible, both as a threat and as an opportunity. Kant believed that it was an unforgivable sin to take a human life, and that the duty to refrain from killing also applies reflexively. For a Kantian, therefore, suicide is out of the question, but Karl Jaspers had

a different attitude to death. He considered death, like birth and sexuality, to be a limit situation, a valuable state of intense existential consciousness. Did these thoughts help Hannah in Gurs?

She certainly seems to have thought about death as a possible solution. In her letter to Kurt, sent in 1952, she explains her reasoning: "In general, things go well; if only world history were not so awful, it would be a joy to live. But, then, that is the case anyway. At least, that was my opinion in Gurs, where I posed the question to myself in earnest and answered myself somewhat jokingly."

The question she asked herself was whether to take her own life, and the conclusion she came to was that suicide as a solution is an answer to an individual problem. Her problem, that she was being held prisoner in a camp while war raged outside, was not an individual problem, however—it was a consequence of other circumstances. Hannah's and the other internees' predicament was the result of historical causes, not individual ones. No part of their situation had to do with any of them as individuals; they were an anonymous collective.

In "We Refugees," Hannah discusses suicide on the basis of an incident that took place in Gurs, when one of her fellow internees suggested collective suicide as an act of protest. Some of the others argued that doing so, choosing death, would be playing into the guards' hands. Wouldn't that be doing exactly what they wanted? Others were struck by a powerful longing to live. Faced with

the sudden possibility of death, life and its value became ever more tangible—just as Jaspers argues. Proximity to death has an impact on a person's perception of life, and when there is a risk of the most profound loss, that also wakes our desire to fight.

HANNAH HAD HAD CAUSE to think about suicide even before she was interned in Gurs. A young man and friend of Walter Benjamin who was held in Villemalard along side Heinrich in the fall of 1939 had taken his own life in the camp. Unlike Heinrich, he was not lucky enough to have been freed. Heinrich had condemned suicide as the coward's way out, as an expression of weakness, but Walter passionately defended the young man's decision, arguing that suicide was an expression of a person's "radical freedom."

Jean-Paul Sartre, who lived in Paris at the same time as Hannah and her friends, argues that through the choices we make, we create our own lives. *That* is our radical freedom. In the book *On Suicide*, Jean Améry, an existentialist like Sartre, claims that suicide is the ultimate expression of this very radical freedom. Améry (whose real name was Hans Mayer) joined the Resistance during the war and was interned at Fort Breendonk in 1943. He was later sent to Auschwitz and was one of very few people who survived—yet he took his own life in 1978.

Walter Benjamin's assertion that suicide is an act of

freedom was one that flourished among the existential-
ists, and it was even glorified by some. Benji had been
toying with the idea of suicide since the outbreak of war,
claiming in spring 1940 that he would prefer a short life
in France to a long life in America. Sadly, that was what
came to pass. On September 26 that same year, Walter
took his own life in the Spanish border town of Portbou.*

"Dear Scholem," Hannah wrote to their mutual friend
Gershom Scholem in fall 1940:

> Walter Benjamin took his own life on September 29
> in Portbou on the Spanish frontier. He had an Amer-
> ican visa, but on the twenty-third the only people the
> Spanish allowed to pass were those with "national"
> passports. I don't know if this letter will reach you.
> In the past weeks and months I had seen Walter
> several times, the last time being on September 20 in
> Marseilles. The report of his death took nearly four
> weeks to reach both his sister and us.
>
> Jews are dying in Europe and are being buried like
> dogs.
>
> Yours,
> Hannah Arendt.

* In the confusion surrounding her and Heinrich's
escape out of France, Hannah believed that the suicide
had actually taken place three days later.

Hannah and Heinrich were shocked by the news of Walter's death. They had assumed he had reached the United States on the visa he had been granted by the American embassy. Since he did not have an exit visa for France, a private American relief organization called the Emergency Rescue Committee had secured him a transit visa to Spain, which would enable him to travel on to Portugal—Walter had a ferry ticket for the America Line, departing from Lisbon. Everything had been prepared, and he and a handful of other refugees crossed the border and reached Portbou, only to be told by border police that they would be deported back to France the next day.

Walter Benjamin checked into a small hotel in the town and ended his life there that same night. The border police were so affected by his death that they allowed the others—those who had been travelling with Walter—to remain in Spain. Walter wrote no suicide note, left no explanation. But, as Hannah wrote in "We Refugees" in 1943, there was no need. The reason was obvious:

> Unlike other suicides, our friends leave no explanation of their deed, no indictment, no charge against a world that had forced a desperate man to talk and to behave cheerfully to his very last day. Letters left by them are conventional, meaningless documents...Nobody cares about motives; they seem to be clear to all of us.

Perhaps Walter had been planning his suicide for some time. Perhaps he had decided to die even before the unfortunate events in Portbou. Perhaps he had simply been waiting for a sign—a final, decisive blow. Walter had fared badly since the outbreak of war. His physical health was weak, and the Gestapo visits to his apartment in Paris had left him tormented, crushed. The Germans had confiscated his books and the texts he had been working on, and his grief at having been robbed of the fundamentals of his life was immense.

Any thinking, writing person could understand his despair. A collection of books is far more than the physical objects: it represents an entire world. The books we read, with exclamation points scrawled in margins, underlined words and folded corners, form an intellectual universe that takes years, possibly even an entire lifetime, to amass. How was Walter expected to start a new library from scratch?

In a letter to Gershom Scholem dated October 17, 1941, Hannah describes how Walter began to talk about suicide almost manically while she was staying with him in Lourdes in the summer of 1940, after she escaped from Gurs: "When news reached us of the first suicide among those in internment fleeing from the Germans, Benjamin began for the first time to talk repeatedly to me about suicide." At the time, of course, Hannah had argued with Walter, telling him that there was plenty of time to escape, that the situation wasn't quite hopeless

yet, that there were other—and better—alternatives.

During their last meeting, Walter had entrusted Hannah and Heinrich with his latest manuscript, "Theses on the Philosophy of History," asking them to take it with them to the United States. Hannah had thought it a slightly odd request, because neither she nor Heinrich had been granted an exit visa from France, whereas Walter had both a visa and a ticket to cross the Atlantic. Why couldn't he simply take the document himself? Still, she and Heinrich had accepted the manuscript and the huge amount of trust Walter was placing in them to deliver it safely to the Institute for Social Research in New York.

Ironically—and tragically—the Spanish border reopened just a few days after Walter Benjamin's suicide. If he had been able to hold out a short while longer, he would have managed to make it to the U.S., to freedom. Many years later, in 1968, Hannah wrote about Walter Benjamin's death in *Men in Dark Times*: "One day earlier Benjamin would have gotten through without any trouble; one day later the people in Marseilles would have known that for the time being it was impossible to pass through Spain. Only on that particular day was the catastrophe possible."

Walter Benjamin, Hannah noted, felt an affinity with Franz Kafka, as evidenced by his words in *Briefe II*: "To do justice to the figure of Kafka in its purity and its peculiar beauty one must never lose sight of one thing: it is the purity and beauty of a failure . . . One is tempted

to say: once he was certain of eventual failure, every-
thing worked out for him *en route* as in a dream." In
her essay on Benjamin, Hannah reasons that Walter's
description of Kafka's vision of himself as a failure was
also a self-description. In his own eyes, he was a failure,
a hopeless case.

Jean Améry, who, like Walter Benjamin, chose to die
by suicide, described his fundamental experience of life
using the term *échec*, which can be translated as "defeat"
or "failure." This was a feeling he lived with long before
he was sent to Auschwitz, but I imagine his sense of
defeat was reinforced by his imprisonment in a concen-
tration camp — much like how Walter Benjamin's vision
of himself and his life as a failure were confirmed on that
fateful day in Portbou, when the border to Spain, the
gateway to freedom and life, was closed to him.

"Hope passed, like a star falling from heaven, over
their heads and away," wrote Goethe. Walter Benjamin
quotes him in an essay, continuing his rumination on
hope in *Schriften I*: "It is only for the sake of those without
hope that hope is given to us." Walter's gasping, faltering
hope abandoned him that night in Portbou.

How does a person cope once they have lost every-
thing? When the darkness is absolute? When death and
evil come between them and the life they want to live?
The answer is hope. It seems crucial to our ability to with-
stand evil, and our only weapon in the fight against giving
in. The capacity to imagine an alternative, something

beyond the present, a time and place that is better than the current moment and current circumstances.

How did Hannah survive? There is no doubt that Hannah understood the importance of hope. In "We Refugees," she wrote the following about the Austrian Jews:

> Since 1938 — since Hitler's invasion of Austria — we have seen how quickly eloquent optimism could change to speechless pessimism. As time went on, we got worse — even more optimistic and even more inclined to suicide. Austrian Jews under Schuschnigg were such a cheerful people — all impartial observers admired them. It was quite wonderful how deeply convinced they were that nothing could happen to them. But when German troops invaded the country and gentile neighbours started riots at Jewish homes, Austrian Jews began to commit suicide.

Yes, Hannah understood the importance of hope. She also possessed the ability to imagine a better future — yet it was her knack for imagining the worst, her suspicious nature, that saved her life on multiple occasions. Hannah never shrugged her shoulders and hoped that things would simply work out. She did not believe that the bad things would go away if she just closed her eyes; she was never so naive. Hannah was able to combine pessimism with an unyielding belief in her own power to change

her circumstances. She left nothing to chance. Hannah always chose to take responsibility, putting duty before the temptation to be drawn into hopelessness.

Twelve

Good and Evil

GOODNESS EXISTS, EVEN IN the darkest of moments. It is worth remembering this — that the violence and brutality of the war did not only bring out the worst in people. The darkness also inspired goodness, bravery, and responsibility. There are countless examples of people who, often at great risk to themselves and their own lives, chose to quietly protest against the violence and cruelty sweeping across Europe. They organized in resistance movements, helping people escape and hiding Jews from the Nazis.

Hannah was one of those brave people who refused to bow to darkness and evil. Before she was forced to leave Germany, she worked secretly to collect evidence of anti-Jewish propaganda. In France, through her work with Youth Aliyah, she helped many Jewish children and teenagers leave Europe for a new life in Mandatory Palestine.

During her years in Paris she also helped Jewish refugees
from Austria and Czechoslovakia find their footing in a
new country. She always did more than she had to. That
is one way of defining goodness: doing more for others
than one is required to do.

Despite this, Hannah herself flinched at the concept
of "goodness," and questioned its place in the political
sphere. In *The Human Condition* (1958), the book in which
she addresses the concept most systematically, she takes
Machiavelli's discussion of goodness as her starting point.
Machiavelli dismisses goodness as political virtue, and
teaches, perhaps deliberately provocatively, the art of
"how not to be good" instead. Of course, this should
not be understood as a rejection of the *personal* virtue of
goodness, by either Machiavelli or Hannah. Instead, it is
an expression of the idea that goodness is not a principle
that has any place within the political sphere. Goodness
is a concept with metaphysical dimensions, a concept
that can much too easily be commandeered by various
religious ideologues and potentates. In essence, Hannah's
hesitant attitude toward goodness as a guiding principle
within politics is a defence of secularism — the idea that
worldly and spiritual affairs should be kept separate.
Religion and religious arguments have no place in polit-
ical, societal discourse.

This is also part of Kant's fundamental approach to
ethics. In the archipelago of thought through which Kant
navigates, goodness, truth, beauty, and other values are

all separate islands. Kant does not champion "goodness"
as the highest value. Instead, he argues that human beings
should act in accordance with goodwill, meaning they
should obey the categorical imperatives: you must not
kill, and you must not lie. According to Kantian ethics,
truth is superior to goodness, simply because truth is
verifiable — in other words, something is either true or
it is false. Goodness, on the other hand, is more a matter
of preference or taste.

In 1988, the Swedish-Finnish writer Willy Kyrklund
illustrated Kant's argument in his typically cutting way,
in an essay titled "On Goodness": "The history of human-
ity shows us that goodness is in constant growth. Ideas
of goodness and demands for goodness have, over the
millennia, come to occupy an ever-greater position in
our imaginations and societies." In his inimitable, gently
mocking style, Kyrklund dissects Western civilization's
obsession with the slippery phenomenon of goodness.
"A good thing," he writes, "can be any old idea or its
material hypostasis. A recognized good thing is anything
considered good by a group of people." Following this
vague statement, he continues with a list of the types of
things that are, or have been considered, good over the
years: "sacred cows, Adolf Hitler, Josef Stalin, Coca-Cola,
sexual abstinence, Hammarby, ice hockey teams, women's
rights, sunbathing, winter bathing, mud baths, showers."

Goodness, Kyrklund goes on, also happens to be of
vital importance in the art of war. In order for a war to

be declared in the first place, at least one side needs to invoke "a good thing." If both parties invoke a reasonable thing, there will be no war, because any conflict of interest can be resolved in a sensible manner. The latter occurs fairly infrequently, however, because reason does not enjoy the same popularity as goodness, and therefore cannot achieve anywhere near the same level of political impact. Thus, the good thing tends to be invoked in place of the reasonable argument, laying the foundations for conflict and war.

In the world of politics in particular, Kyrklund writes sarcastically, goodness is an imperative; it is the chief requirement for political success. Every dictator needs a following that will celebrate him as a god, paving the way to power. Hand on heart, who would ever vote for an evil person? "Fortunately," Kyrklund continues, "the supply of good people is plentiful."

Things have scarcely changed since Kyrklund came to this conclusion. Yes, the "good" are growing in number, while the reasonable continue to decline. There are also more wars and intractable conflicts, through which the good thing must be defended while reason is relegated to the corner. Once goodness has begun to develop, as Kyrklund writes, it cannot be stopped. It soon detaches itself from any connection to the individual's own welfare; it becomes detached from interests of survival and becomes idealism.

The good person fights for a good thing, and therefore

anyone who protests against this — thereby promoting "bad" things — is a bad person. "It is easy to see the importance of idealism to morale in the army," Kyrklund writes. The war for the good never ends — there are always enemies of the good that must be fought, whatever the cost. Indeed, goodness is hard to argue with. Goodness is, in Kyrklund's opinion, arbitrary, and to say that something good is bad implies from the very outset a *contradictio in adiecto*, a self-contradiction.

Hannah never read Kyrklund's scathing essay on goodness, of course, but she likely would have appreciated it. In a letter to William O'Grady, a student who took part in her seminars in Chicago during the 1960s, she expresses a similar position toward "goodness" and "good people." In his original letter to Hannah, the young student describes his efforts to be a "very good person," to which she replies: "I don't quite know what you mean when you say 'good,' but I know that the wish to be 'good' is an even greater temptation than the wish to be 'wise.' That is precisely what we cannot *be*."

In her essay on Bertolt Brecht, published in *Men in Dark Times* in 1968, Hannah presents a similar argument based on Brecht's understanding of the lure of goodness: *Schrecklich ist die Verführung zur Güte* — "terrible is the temptation to be good." As Kant argued, if there is such a thing as a temptation to do evil, there is also a temptation to do good. And not just that, Hannah writes: there is also a temptation to *be* good. In her essay on Brecht,

she describes his attempts to be a good person—attempts which ultimately led to him doing evil deeds instead.

There had been a time when Hannah admired Brecht. During her years in Paris, he was considered almost a martyr in the circles in which she moved, a hero who had been forced to leave Germany because of his political convictions. Compared to the intellectuals who had disappointed Hannah after Hitler's rise to power, Brecht was admirable, someone who stood up for his beliefs and refused to bow to authority.

The poem Walter Benjamin had brought back to Paris after his visit to Brecht in Svendborg had provided both Hannah and Heinrich with comfort and courage while they were interned and separated from each other. But Brecht's behaviour after the war, once Germany was divided between East and West, and once the capital, Berlin, was split in two, did not impress Hannah.

His crime was not, Hannah writes, that he was a communist during the 1920s and '30s—being a communist in Europe at that time was more a mistake than a sin. No, his crime was that he persevered in his beliefs even once he settled in East Berlin, where he could see with his own eyes the impact communism was having on the people. Hannah's disappointment in Brecht is tangible in her essay. He should have known better.

After the end of the war and his years in exile in Scandinavia and the United States, Bertolt Brecht moved back to Europe. Life had become uncomfortable for him

in America. In 1947, he was interrogated by the House Un-American Activities Committee about his relationship with communism and the Soviet Union. Shortly after this, he travelled to Zurich, Switzerland, before ultimately settling in East Berlin in 1949. There, against his better judgement, he chose to remain loyal to the communist regime. In her essay on Brecht, Hannah writes that he was perfectly aware of Stalin's ravages and the failures of communism, but that his revolutionary dreams led him astray. Brecht understood from an early stage that communism demanded evil deeds in order to achieve its ultimate aim, the workers' utopia: "He had scarcely joined the Communists before he found out that in order to change the bad world into a good world it was not enough 'not to be good' but that you had to become bad yourself, that in order to exterminate meanness there should be no mean thing you were not ready to do."

Brecht was manipulated by an evil system that claimed to be good, a system that claimed to treat everyone the same way, but which in reality repressed them and kept them shackled in poverty. In *Me-ti, Buch der Wendungen*, published after his death, Brecht self-mockingly describes a suitable punishment for the good man who has lost his way:

So listen: we know
You are our enemy. That's why we now want

To stand you against a wall. But considering your
 services
And good qualities
Against a good wall and shoot you with
Good bullets from good rifles and bury you with
A good shovel in good earth.

Hannah could not bear sanctimonious people, those
who wore their goodness like a uniform, showing off
their good deeds as though they were gemstones. In
The Human Condition, she draws a connection to Jesus'
sermons on good deeds. "The one activity taught by
Jesus in word and deed is the activity of goodness, and
goodness obviously harbours a tendency to hide from
being seen or heard. Christian hostility toward the public
realm, the tendency at least of early Christians to lead
a life as far removed from the public realm as possible,
can also be understood as a self-evident consequence of
devotion to good works, independent of all beliefs and
expectations," she writes, finding support for her belief
that politics and religion, society and the church, should
be kept separate.

"For it is manifest that the moment a good work
becomes known and public, it loses its specific character
of goodness, of being done for nothing but goodness'
sake. When goodness appears openly, it is no longer
goodness, though it may still be useful as organized
charity or an act of solidarity," she continues, concluding

that goodness exists only when it is performed *not* as goodness. "Whoever sees himself performing a good work is no longer good," she writes, almost as an echo of Kant.

Kant's requirement for absolute altruism is very strict, possibly too strict—after all, an act that has good consequences is, in all likelihood, good, whether the person carrying it out praises themselves for doing good or not. When assessing the moral value of an act, we can start either from the intention of the person carrying out the act or from the consequences of the act itself. As a deontological, duty-based ethicist, Kant argues that it is the intention that counts in the assessment of the moral value of an act, but the weakness of this approach is that it is incredibly difficult to assess a person's intention. The alternative, therefore, is to assess the consequences rather than the intention.

But then we must also consider exactly which consequences we mean—the immediate consequences, or more long-term? Direct or indirect? Furthermore, we must ask who is included in our moral considerations—meaning, consequences for whom? For me? For my family? For everyone in my country? For everyone on earth? In the assessment of the moral value of an act—is it good or evil, right or wrong—we must therefore use reason rather than rely on our emotional reactions.

After all, morality is not primarily a matter of emotions. Considering ethical dilemmas and moral

problems demands reason and rationality. We must argue rather than feel.

The antidote to evil is not, as one might instinctively assume, goodness, even if good and evil are each other's antithesis. Hannah argues that the antidote is reflection and responsibility. When people cease to think, reflect, and choose between good and evil, between taking part or resisting, that is when evil grows. In *Responsibility and Judgment* she writes of the risks in viewing the philosophical statement that "nobody does evil voluntarily" as a reasonable description of human nature; the statement leads to another assumption, namely that "everybody wants to do good." The sad truth, Hannah writes, is that evil deeds are typically carried out by people who have not made a decision to be good or evil. They have simply not chosen a side.

Thirteen

A New Beginning

IN THE FALL OF 1940, Hannah and Heinrich had real-
ized that the time to flee had come. But they needed
help, and that was where Varian Fry came in. Fry was
an American journalist who, having experienced anti-
Semitism and Nazism during his time as a correspondent
in Berlin in 1935, made the decision to save as many Jews
and intellectuals as he could. With the support and
backing of First Lady Eleanor Roosevelt, he created the
Emergency Rescue Committee, an underground network
in Marseilles; and he was, along with Miriam Davenport
and Mary Jayne Gold, the spider at the heart of the web.
The group collaborated closely with the U.S. consulate
in Marseilles.

At the time, Hiram Bingham IV was vice consul in
Marseilles, and he personally issued thousands of visas,
both legal and illegal, to those who needed to escape

France. The Emergency Rescue Committee managed to help many thousands of Jews and anti-Nazi intellectuals leave France and find safety in the United States. Hannah and Heinrich were among the first to be granted emergency visas by the American consulate. Thanks to Hannah's visa gained because of her work with Youth Aliyah, and the couple's foresight in getting married while they still could, Heinrich was also granted a visa.

Hannah and Heinrich's journey to freedom began in Marseilles. They biked from Montauban to the large port city in late October 1940, a journey that took twenty-four hours of solid cycling, to pick up the documents that would permit them to leave the country. Exhausted and hungry, they arrived under the cover of darkness and checked into a hotel. Their escape could easily have come to an abrupt end right there, because early the next morning, a message was sent up to their room urging Heinrich to report to reception at once. The couple realized that they were in danger — that the police were hot on their heels — and they acted quickly, almost instinctively. Heinrich calmly went down to the lobby, placed his key on the reception desk, and left the hotel before anyone spotted him. Shortly after this, Hannah followed him down to the café they had chosen as their rendezvous point. Once they were sure that Heinrich was safe and that no one was following him, Hannah returned to the hotel to collect their belongings, eat breakfast, and pay for their room.

As she sat in the dining room, eating toast, drinking chicory coffee, and attempting to look calm, the receptionist came over to her table to ask where Heinrich was. The receptionist was clearly following police orders, and Hannah realized that she would have to convince her that Heinrich had already gone. With all the dramatic flair she could muster, she caused a scene, shouting that her husband had already reported to the station and that she held the receptionist personally responsible for his safety. The act worked: the startled woman apologized, and returned to her seat behind the desk in the lobby.

Once Hannah and Heinrich were reunited at the café, they immediately left Marseilles with their precious documents. Hannah's mother, Martha, had not yet been granted an emergency visa, but following their unpleasant experience at the hotel, Hannah and Heinrich realized they would have to leave without her. Hannah asked her friend Nina Gourfinkel, who was in Montauban distributing Swiss food parcels and American emergency packages to the many refugees there, to look after Martha. Leaving so abruptly was by no means an easy decision for Hannah, but with Nina's promise to take care of Martha until she too was granted a visa for the United States, she felt slightly reassured.

Just as Hannah had predicted, the French police came to work alongside the SS in their hunt for Jews, members of the Resistance, and communists. During

the summer and fall of 1942, 27,000 stateless Jews were deported to Auschwitz, 18,000 of them from Paris and 9,000 from Vichy France. From January 22 to 24, 1943, the French police carried out a joint raid with the SS on the Jewish population of Marseilles. Twelve thousand police officers, brought in from across France, searched house after house; 1,500 buildings were destroyed, and 40,000 identities checked. The result was that 6,000 people were arrested, and 4,000 were sent to internment camps in Drancy and Compiègne before being transported to German concentration camps. The French police's collaboration with the Nazis cost many Jews their lives.

How much did the French people understand of what was happening? Were they aware of the dangers facing Jews and those who, like Heinrich, had been forced to flee Germany because of their political beliefs? They knew that the Vichy regime was pro-German, of course, but perhaps they did not realize the scope of what was going on.

Hannah and Heinrich made sure they were ready to leave as soon as an opportunity arose. Their bags were packed and their documents—their emergency visas and tickets for the passage that would take them to America, funded by the Jewish organization HIAS, the Hebrew Immigrant Aid Society—kept safe. They pored over every newspaper they could get their hands on, listening to radio broadcasts in order to work out

the optimum time to depart. In early January 1941, such a moment finally arose: the Vichy regime temporarily relaxed its strict exit rules, and Hannah and Heinrich took the first train to Portbou, the Spanish border town where Walter Benjamin had ended his own life just a few months earlier. From there, they would continue on, toward Lisbon.

Nestled at the foot of the Pyrenees, Portbou was a small town that had suffered greatly during the Spanish Civil War. Half the town's inhabitants died during the bloody conflict that tore through Spain between 1936 and 1939, culminating in Franco's seizure of power, and in 1941, the town was still in a state of disrepair. There had been neither the time, money, nor energy to rebuild any of the damaged buildings.

During the civil war, many Republicans had escaped Franco by crossing the mountains into France, via Portbou. Some ended up in Gurs, the internment camp Hannah had managed to escape from. By the Second World War, however, Portbou had become a route *into* Spain, for those fleeing the Nazis and heading to Portugal to make the onward journey to the United States or Palestine. An estimated 40,000 Jewish refugees crossed the French-Spanish border between 1940 and 1941, the vast majority heading for Portugal.

The town's cemetery, carved into the mountain-side, is located in a small bay, with the ocean its closest neighbour. Hannah and Heinrich made their way here

in search of Walter's grave, and Hannah described the
visit in a letter to Gershom Scholem:

> When we arrived at Portbou, we searched in vain for
> his grave. It was nowhere to be found. His name was
> nowhere. The cemetery looks off at a small bay, directly
> onto the Mediterranean. It is composed of terraces
> carved out of stone. The coffins are shoved into these
> stone walls. It is by far one of the most fantastically
> beautiful places I've ever seen.

After a few days in Portbou, Hannah and Heinrich set off
for Lisbon, the Portuguese capital. In the 1940s, Portugal
was still a relatively poor country. It remained neutral
throughout the war, but the prime minister, António
Salazar, allowed thirty-day tourist visas for those fleeing
Germany — despite holding pro-Nazi views himself. He
sympathized with the German National Socialists and
feared that "Jewish communists" would cause political
and social unrest. Salazar allowed Jewish refugees to pass
through his country, but only so that they could reach
Lisbon, the gateway out of Europe, and then leave the
continent.

Tens of thousands sought refuge in neutral Portugal,
both Jews and non-Jews alike. With its illuminated
streets, late-night cafés, and bustling street life, Lisbon
must have seemed like an oasis for those fleeing intern-
ment, curfews, and air-raid warnings. Antoine de

Saint-Exupéry, the French author of *The Little Prince*, among other works, described the atmosphere there, writing, "In 1940 Lisbon, happiness was staged so that God could believe it still existed."

Some of the more well-off refugees could afford to buy tickets for the "flying ships"—the Pan American Airways flights departing Europe for America twice a week—but the majority had nowhere near enough money. For them, the only option was to board one of the ships crossing the Atlantic, heading for destinations like Havana, Philadelphia, Baltimore, New York, and Rio de Janeiro. Getting hold of a ticket for one of these passages was far from easy, however, as the only boats able to leave the harbour without facing the risk of being torpedoed were those sailing under the flags of neutral countries like Portugal and the U.S.

The Portuguese people were not uniformly happy about their country being used as a transit corridor for those fleeing the war. The refugees spent their days sitting in Lisbon's cafés, drinking coffee, smoking, and talking. Pastelaria Suiça, on Rossio Square, became a meeting place for those living in exile, in waiting. They met there not simply to socialize, but to barter for tickets to suitable destinations. The Portuguese, many of them devout Catholics, looked on with distaste at the often more fashionable refugees and their clothing and manners—particularly the Jewish women, who not only smoked in public, but drank wine and laughed loudly.

Hannah and Heinrich mostly kept to themselves. They found a small apartment in a green building in a quiet area of the city, on Rua da Sociedade Farmacêutica, and spent their days talking, reading, and waiting. At first, they were waiting for Hannah's mother to arrive, but before long they began to bide their time for two of the sought-after places on one of the boats crossing the Atlantic. They read aloud to each other from the manuscript Walter Benjamin had entrusted them with, his "Theses on the Philosophy of History." Perhaps they thought back to the time they had spent with him in the countryside, to the happy days just before the war began.

On May 10, after almost four months in Lisbon, their turn to board a ship finally came. Martha had been promised a place on another liner, departing Lisbon ten days later, and so, on the SS *Guiné*, a freighter refitted as a passenger ship, Hannah and Heinrich left Europe, the continent they had always called home. It would be years before either of them would be able to return.

What was Hannah thinking as the SS *Guiné* left the harbour, and Europe, setting off into unknown waters, toward a country—a continent—she had never visited before? She hints at the answer in "We Refugees":

We lost our home, which means the familiarity of daily life. We lost our occupation, which means the confidence that we are of some use in this world. We lost our language, which means the naturalness of reactions,

the simplicity of gestures, the unaffected expression of feelings. We left our relatives in the Polish ghettos and our best friends have been killed in concentration camps, and that means the rupture of our private lives.

Hannah lost everything — her home, her language, her occupation, her relatives and friends, her place in the world, both geographically and existentially; all this had been taken from her, and the voyage across the Atlantic was not simply the journey to a new country, but to a new life. Above all, it was a journey away from the evil that was ravaging Europe, away from the threat of internment or death. Hannah did not leave Europe in search of a better life — she had already inhabited the very life she wanted. No, she left because that life and the existence she loved had been taken from her. She was not making her way *to* something, but *away* from something. Hannah fled in order to save her life, not because she wanted a new one.

Fourteen

"Without a Place to Call My Own"

HANNAH AND HEINRICH ARRIVED in the United States on May 22, 1941, each with a suitcase and twenty-five dollars in their pocket. They were granted a monthly allowance of seventy dollars by an American Zionist organization, and found a small, partly furnished apartment to rent on West 95th Street in New York, where they settled to wait for Hannah's mother to arrive. The SS *Muzinho* docked in New York on June 21, and the family of three tried to find a way to coexist in their tiny, sparse flat.

Hannah was in her thirty-fifth year and Heinrich his forty-third when they arrived in New York. They had been living in exile in France for many years, getting to know a new country, moving between apartments and cities; they had been interned and on the run, hiding,

losing good friends and family members, leaving others behind. But finally, *finally*, they had found safety. How must it feel to arrive in a country you have never visited before, with a language you do not speak and a culture you do not understand? I am sure it must be quite frustrating, though also a relief of sorts. Hannah and Heinrich had started over before, in France — learning the language and creating a life for themselves, with friends and work. Now it was time to do the same again.

In "We Refugees," published in the *Menorah Journal* in January 1943, Hannah wrote about her experience of being a refugee roughly a year and a half after arriving in the United States. The tone is blunt, honest, rebellious, and frustrated. She does not want to be thought of as a victim, does not want to be given charity, does not want to be called a refugee. Hannah describes the anxiety, the fear, and the struggle to exist — the struggle for the right to be seen as an individual rather than part of an anonymous mass of "refugees." She fights for dignity and for the ability to create an independent life of her own, and she also describes the sense of alienation she feels with respect to both her new country, America, and her new identity as a refugee. The text begins with something of a manifesto:

> In the first place, we don't like to be called "refugees." We ourselves call each other "newcomers" or "immigrants" . . . A refugee used to be a person driven to seek

refuge because of some act committed or some polit-
ical opinion held. Well, it is true we have had to seek
refuge; but we committed no acts and most of us never
dreamt of having any radical political opinion. With us
the meaning of the term "refugee" has changed. Now
"refugees" are those of us who have been so unfortu-
nate as to arrive in a new country without means and
have to be helped by refugee committees.

There is no mistaking Hannah's frustration at the
helplessness inherent in being a refugee. She resists
being defined as a victim, as someone who needs help,
the object of other people's pity, while at the same time
understanding that that is precisely what she is: a person
who has been forced to flee as a result of unjust persecu-
tion, and who therefore has to rely on the help of others
to navigate her new existence. She seems to defend
herself against the perception of being weak, of being
dependent on others. Hannah was used to being strong,
the kind of person who took care of others, not someone
who needed to be taken care of herself.

In July 1941, Hannah travelled to the small town of
Winchester, Massachusetts, a sleepy, well-off commun-
ity around eight miles north of Boston. Heinrich and
Martha remained in New York. Through the Self-Help
for Refugees agency, Hannah had been given an oppor-
tunity to improve her English by spending a month living
with an American family. Her hosts would provide food,

board, and conversation, in exchange for various chores around the house.

In a number of long letters, she described her stay to Heinrich, giving expression to mixed feelings. In the first letter, dated July 21, she writes that the host couple, Mr. and Mrs. Giduz, prepared for her arrival by buying an English–German dictionary and making up a bedroom for her. Their compassion left a real impression on Hannah, yet she cannot help but describe them as two fairly ridiculous characters:

> He tries his hardest to do his best with me, and has the dark notion that I'm superior to him, and the very American fear of being made fun of. Good sense of humor. His wife hovers in the fear that I could take something amiss or think that they might be trying to exploit me. This is the height of comedy. For I help them exactly as much or as little as I would help any friends I stay with. And this even if they protest.

Power plays a role in all human relationships: who has the ability to create, maintain, or break the relationship—both parties, or only one? Hannah was still sensitive to power and hierarchies, and she detested feeling powerless. At a very crude level, relationships can be categorized as asymmetrical or symmetrical, and the relationship she shared with the Giduzes was fundamentally asymmetrical. In a symmetrical relationship, the

two parties are equal, and possess the same degree of power to shape the relationship. In an asymmetrical relationship, however, there is a power imbalance of some kind—A possesses the power because B is, in one way or another, in a dependent position. B becomes an object of either exploitation or care.

For a proud person like Hannah, being reduced to an object was unbearable. She wanted to regain power over her own life, taking charge of her circumstances, but she knew that in order to be able to do this, she would have to come to understand the language, culture, and people of the country that had given her sanctuary.

In a later letter, Hannah writes that she is "quite glad I decided to try this experiment. I'm learning a lot, even more about this country than about the language. It isn't exactly comforting. Newspapers and radio speeches here are giving a totally false picture, particularly when it comes to opinions on the war."

Mr. and Mrs. Giduz were both pacifists. Hannah describes Mrs. Giduz in particular as "against all war, and definitely prepared to climb the barricades to fight for that." She goes on to say that Mrs. Giduz is "also ready to fight to the death for healthy nutrition. Healthy nutrition is: 1. No meat. 2. No fried fat (gallbladder diet). 3. Lots of vegetables, preferably raw. 4. No white bread." Hannah, in other words, had ended up with a couple of vegetarian pacifists, who were repulsed by nicotine and spent their weekends birdwatching.

This was something of a culture shock to Hannah, who was a seasoned smoker, had spent much of the past few years hungry, and thought the United States should declare war on Germany. Her American hosts' attitudes and lifestyle perplexed her, but she viewed everything through a scientific lens, and, as she wrote to Heinrich, learned a lot about her new country and its people.

When Hannah and Heinrich first arrived in the United States, the nation had not yet joined the war in Europe. Their new homeland was still struggling to get back on its feet after the crisis of the 1930s. The 1929 stock market crash had brought an abrupt end to the decadent, carefree twenties—the decade in which jazz music hit the mainstream, women cut their hair short, and people had time to go to the movies and listen to the radio. Ironically, the roaring twenties had coincided with the Prohibition era, during which the production, import, and sale of alcohol was banned in the U.S. Underground clubs began to flourish as a result, enabling people to drink and dance; after the suffering of the First World War, they wanted to have fun. By the end of the decade, however, that free and easy attitude had evaporated.

The stock market crash was followed by financial crisis, deepened by the fact that the technological advances of the era were making workers increasingly superfluous. As machines began to replace people, unemployment levels shot up, and that in turn reduced people's buying power. Reduced buying power meant

that various industries struggled to sell products and were consequently forced to let more of their workers go.

In 1933, President Franklin D. Roosevelt launched a program of reform known as the New Deal, aiming to reduce unemployment and drag the nation out of crisis. By providing support for industry and farming, investing in the public sector, and building roads, it helped people back into work, increasing their spending power and enabling them to become consumers again. When the program was launched, 15 million Americans were out of work. By 1937, this had fallen to 7 million, and by 1941 the figure was even lower.

The Giduz family, Hannah's hosts in Massachusetts, were among the millions of ordinary Americans who had been badly affected by the financial crash. On July 28, Hannah wrote to Heinrich:

> Thursday evening, Madam told me that her husband had been unemployed a good eleven years and had almost gone crazy. And that, even though with her earnings they had enough to live on, and for the car, and to pay off the house. The effects of unemployment are exactly the same as we know them, even when there is no immediate danger of starving. He refused to eat, and things like that. She was often at the point of running off. And couldn't have children, a real hurt. Even though he has an above-average interest in all kinds of things, for years he just slept.

To lose one's job and be left without context is a profoundly depressing experience. When a person loses their context, they also lose the foundation of their very existence. "Hundreds of thousands of families over here went through the same thing, and one can't understand this country if one doesn't constantly keep the factor of unemployment and joblessness in view," she went on. By the time Hannah arrived in Winchester, Mr. Giduz had finally found work, but the terms of his employment were very insecure; he could lose his job from one day to the next.

Perhaps Hannah's heart softened slightly with this new knowledge about the Giduzes, about whom she had been slightly scathing earlier: "I was very impressed by the story, especially by the fact that the moment things got slightly better she immediately began helping a refugee, feeling that she had to do something as quickly as possible. Great, isn't it?"

Once Mrs. Giduz revealed her and her husband's disadvantages, they immediately came to be on a more equal footing with Hannah. The power imbalance lessened. They were all, in their own way, victims of circumstances over which they had no control, and they all struggled to regain their standing, to master their fate, and to recover their pride.

Fifteen

The Maiden from Afar

HANNAH FOUGHT TO CREATE a new life for herself in the United States, though she also longed for the life she had been forced to leave behind. She was plagued by homesickness—a longing that never quite diminished, however much she came to love America. But what, exactly, was she longing for?

In a conversation with Karl Jaspers, Hannah once insisted that she was not German. He had corrected her, arguing that of course she was, but as Hannah later told Günter Gaus: "I...don't believe that I have ever considered myself German—in the sense of belonging to the people as opposed to being a citizen." She felt like Friedrich von Schiller's *Mädchen aus der Fremde*. That was what Heinrich called her, too. The maiden from afar.

Despite this, Hannah longed to return home for the rest of her life. Perhaps it was a state or a time she missed,

rather than any physical location—the Europe in which she grew up and became an adult? In her interview with Gaus, Hannah discussed her relationship with Europe and with language—with German, *die Muttersprache*. "The German language is the essential thing that has remained," she told him. Being surrounded by one's language: that is being at home. Language represents continuity, and the German language was Hannah's home. After all, as she explained in that interview in 1964: "It wasn't the German language that went crazy." The country may have been lost to Hannah, but the German language would remain her home until death.

The poet and Nobel Prize winner Nelly Sachs— who, like Hannah, was forced to leave her homeland in order to save her life—writes the following in the poem "Someone Comes": "A stranger always has / his home- land in his arms / like an orphan / for which he may be seeking / nothing but a grave."

When Nelly Sachs penned those words at the end of the Second World War, her motherland no longer existed. After 1944, neither she nor Hannah had a European home. Hannah was by then living in the United States, and Nelly in Sweden, the country to which she had fled in 1940. The Jewish people had been expelled from Germany. An incomprehensible number of them had been slaughtered.

In 1946, Hannah wrote about her sorrow and her long- ing for the home that no longer existed:

Sorrow is like a light that gleams in the heart,
Darkness is a glow that searches our night.
We need strike only the small, mournful flame
To find our way home, like shadows, through the
 long, broad night.
The woods, the city, the street, the tree are
 luminous.
Lucky is he who has no home; he sees it still in his
 dreams.

Perhaps Hannah was making a reference to Friedrich Nietzsche's verse here? He not only wrote philosophical texts; like Hannah, he also wrote poetry. One of his most famous poems, "Vereinsamt," contains the lines *"Wohl dem, der jetzt noch — Heimat hat"* and *"Weh dem, der keine Heimat hat."* In English: "Happy is he who still — has a home" and "Woe unto him who has no home," respectively. Nietzsche gives expression to the same wistful attitude to the motherland and love for the native country as both Hannah Arendt and Nelly Sachs.

But what is a homeland, a hometown? A place you recognize, a place where you feel at home, a place where you are among friends, a place where you feel safe. All this was taken from Hannah — and Nelly Sachs. The place they thought was theirs never really existed. "Lucky is he who has no home; he sees it still in his dreams," Hannah wrote. As for Nelly Sachs, she was searching for

a grave in which to place her burden — the burden of the homeland she carried in her arms.

Hannah had grown up in Königsberg, the East Prussian city which, after the end of the war, was annexed by the Soviet Union and became known as Kaliningrad, but her family ties to the city stretched back no further than a few generations. In this, Hannah's family history is not unique. Many of the Jewish refugees who arrived in the U.S. as a result of the Second World War had moved from country to country, and no longer had a place to call home. Indeed, as Hannah remarks in one of the letters she sent to Heinrich from Winchester, while she was staying with the Giduz family, the same was true of many Americans, too. Their relationship with their country was not a long-standing one, and they were greatly preoccupied with their origins: "Here, three generations later you are still what your forefathers were. The lady of the house tells me, for instance, that the other day a Swede came into her office — and his parents were born here!"

Sixteen

The End of the War

HANNAH WAS PARTICULARLY ANNOYED by what she considered to be the inaccurate image of the war in Europe painted by the American media: "Basically no one wants the war, and no one comprehends it or can understand even slightly what it's all about," she wrote in a letter to Heinrich from Winchester.

The American people, finally emerging from a deep economic depression, were not particularly enthusiastic about being drawn into another war—especially not one taking place on another continent.

But that wouldn't last. On December 7, 1941, just a few months after Hannah left the Giduz family in Winchester and returned to New York to be reunited with Heinrich and her mother, everything changed. Early that morning, the Japanese Navy Air Service attacked the United States naval base at Pearl Harbor,

on the island of Oahu, Hawaii. Three hundred and fifty-three Japanese bombers bore down on the base, sinking several ships and destroying 188 American planes. There were 2,402 fatalities, and a further 1,282 people were injured.

The attack came as a shock to the American people, and their previously strong support for the country's isolationist strategy—for keeping the United States out of the war—vanished. The day after the attack on Pearl Harbor, the country declared war on Japan, dragging the U.S. into the conflict. The Japanese strike on the American naval base was a so-called surprise attack, undertaken without any warning, in violation of both international law and established "good practice." In an address to the nation, President Roosevelt described December 7 as "a date which will live in infamy."

The background to the attack on Pearl Harbor was the fact that the United States, in collaboration with the U.K. and the Netherlands, had frozen all Japanese commercial assets in an attempt to prevent the country's expansion into Southeast Asia—and in support of China in its war against Japan. At the time of the unannounced Japanese attack, the country was in negotiations with the United States, which was demanding that Japan withdraw from China and leave the Tripartite Pact, signed by Germany, Italy, and Japan in September 1940. Japan was clearly unwilling to agree to those terms, and had chosen instead to attack Pearl Harbor in the hope that

taking out the United States' Pacific fleet would force the U.S. to negotiate for peace.

Because Japan was a member of the Tripartite Pact, Roosevelt's declaration of war was, in practice, also a declaration of war against Germany and Italy, as well as the other signatories: Hungary, Romania, Slovakia, Bulgaria, Yugoslavia, and Croatia. The three Axis powers, along with the other countries in the pact, had promised to support and help one another if attacked by a foreign power. As a result, the remaining countries rushed to Japan's defence. Just three days after Roosevelt's declaration of war, Hitler announced that Germany would fight on Japan's side.

Ironically, it was the United States' entry into the war that dragged the country out of its financial crisis. With the nation's men leaving for the front, its women joined the workforce, and the economy enjoyed a powerful upswing thanks to the sudden demand for airplanes and tanks. Even the entertainment industry saw an impact: Mickey Mouse and Superman were recruited, the Andrews Sisters entertained the American troops with swing and boogie-woogie, and Marilyn Monroe experienced her big breakthrough.

Nineteen-year-old Monroe, who still went by the name Norma Jeane at the time, was discovered in 1944 by a photographer visiting the munitions factory where she worked. The images of the scantily clad, smiling young woman were incredibly popular among the soldiers, who

covered the walls of their cabins and barracks with pin-ups. Pictures of Marilyn, like many other curvy women, were reproduced on bomber planes as so-called nose art girls. Society's permissive attitude toward shorter skirts, low-cut tops, provocative dancing, and suggestive lyrics were all expressions of solidarity with the young men who had gone off to war. Immorality was, quite simply, necessary to keep up morale; all those young men so far from home needed cheering up. But the war years were a mere parenthesis—the years that followed the end of the conflict were particularly prudish. The conservative family values of the 1950s were completely at odds with the relative abandon of the 1940s.

WITH THE WAR EVER-PRESENT in the background, Hannah and Heinrich continued in their struggle to find work, income, and context. Hannah, who found learning English easier than Heinrich did, was more successful in establishing herself. She turned to the Zion-ist circles in New York, and through her contacts there found work writing columns for the German-language journal *Aufbau*, distributed to German-speaking refugees across the world.

Writing in German was not entirely uncontroversial in New York's intellectual circles at the time. The influ-ential political philosopher Leo Strauss recommended, for example, that no Jew should have anything to do with

Germany going forward. He, like the group of academics and authors around him, argued that anything linked to Germany should be boycotted, including its philosophy, literature, music, and art — even its language. Hannah did not believe in collective guilt, neither then nor later, and maintained her relationship with Germany, above all through the language.

Heinrich was struck by a deep sense of melancholy, a grief at the state of the world and his own inability to contribute to improving it, almost to the point that he became catatonic. Without either the language or a formal education, he was unable to make a living doing the same kind of intellectual work he had in Europe. In America, he was nothing.

For Martha, this simply reinforced her belief that the man her daughter had married was good for nothing. It isn't hard to imagine what the atmosphere must have been like in the cramped New York apartment they shared. Three people, all trying to find their place in a new country, trying to understand a new language and culture as war raged around the world and the friends and family they had left behind were in constant danger.

Martha, who was sixty-seven when she arrived in the United States, took care of things around the house, cooking for her little family — not an insignificant task, given their lack of funds and a kitchen of their own; the tenants in their building shared both a kitchen and a bathroom. Martha felt isolated and struggled to learn

English, and the anxiety that had developed during the war years refused to let go.

Then, finally, the war ended. On May 8, 1945, word reached Hannah and Heinrich that Germany had capitulated and Hitler was dead.

It was a ravaged Europe that celebrated the end of the fighting. The people of Paris, London, and Amsterdam danced on the streets against a backdrop of bombed-out buildings. Close to 80 million people had died as a result of the war, and around 6 million Jews had been murdered. Millions of people had lost everything they owned, and the scope of material and economic destruction was huge. Europe's industries had been bombed and destroyed. And yet, the people celebrated. The war was finally over.

Celebration reigned in the United States, too. President Harry Truman dedicated the day, May 8, to his predecessor, Franklin D. Roosevelt, who had died on April 12 that same year, less than a month before VE Day. Hannah and Heinrich were staying with good friends in Connecticut when the news reached them, and they toasted with champagne, dearly hoping they would finally be able to re-establish contact with those who had remained in Europe. Before long, they began to receive letters from France, and to Hannah's great joy, she discovered that Anne Mendelsohn Weil, one of her oldest friends, was still alive. Anne had worked with the French Resistance during the war, and her husband, Éric, had been held in

various German prison camps. Both had survived.

In September 1945, Hannah received another letter that filled her with joy: Karl Jaspers, with whom she had not been in contact since she fled Germany in 1933, wrote to her via U.S. military mail. For Hannah, the letter from Jaspers became a link to her past, to the life and the country — the Germany — that had once been hers.

Seventeen

The Right to Have Rights

EIGHTEEN LONG YEARS AFTER Hannah escaped Germany, she finally became an American citizen. Not until 1951 did she find a place, a people, to belong to, and a country that would protect her. Hannah's political philosophy was shaped during her stateless years, when she existed without the rights that citizenship provides an individual. It is perhaps surprising, therefore, that she was openly skeptical toward the idea of universal human rights. In *The Origins of Totalitarianism*, she writes, with a certain acidity:

> We became aware of the existence of a right to have rights (and that means to live in a framework where one is judged by one's actions and opinions) and a right to belong to some kind of organized community, only when millions of people emerged who had lost and

could not regain these rights because of the new global
political situation... The right that corresponds to this
loss and that was never even mentioned among the
human rights cannot be expressed in the categories
of the eighteenth century because they presume that
rights spring immediately from the "nature" of man...
the right to have rights, or the right of every individ-
ual to belong to humanity, should be guaranteed by
humanity itself.

In this passage, Hannah refers to the historic discussion
of human rights as a given, as a natural consequence
of some kind of essential human nature. The issue she
takes with this approach is that it treats people as though
they were nothing but substance, simply objects. It does
not provide a sufficient definition of humankind. In
Hannah's opinion, humans are beings with the capacity
for questioning themselves—conscious beings—and it
is only in relation to these qualities that we can argue for
the right to have rights. Human rights are guaranteed
neither by history, such as by the Magna Carta, as was
argued following the Glorious Revolution of 1688, nor
by nature, as the Enlightenment philosophers claimed.
Only humankind, Hannah argues, can guarantee human
rights to others.

Hannah also refers to the long-discussed concept of
human dignity—what is it, exactly, that gives human-
kind its worth? The term "human dignity" is typically

used to assert that individuals have an intrinsic value, and that they are assigned this simply by virtue of being people. Since everyone possesses this same value, everyone is therefore equal. It is this conviction that guarantees us human rights — they stem directly from the principle of human dignity.

In Western history, human dignity has often been justified through either religious beliefs or qualifications. The theologically motivated arguments for human dignity revolve around the idea of *Imago Dei*, or the image of God. Since humankind is created in God's image, it has infinite, inviolable value. Hannah did not believe in God, and she therefore understood human dignity in relation to human qualities instead. She chose to focus on consciousness, adopting the Platonic, Aristotelian tradition.

As early as 1486, in a text entitled *Oration on the Dignity of Man*, Giovanni Pico della Mirandola asserted the unique worth and rights of humankind. He cited human worth in its nature and characteristics: humans are free and responsible, and therefore possess particular rights. Unfortunately, the notion that humans have special rights does not prevent them from behaving cruelly toward one another, as Hannah points out. Human rights are not like metaphysics or ideology; human dignity must be demonstrated through concrete acts, by fellow beings of flesh and blood.

In practice, there is no human dignity if we do not bring it into being through our actions. Hannah

understood this, and argued that only humans can guarantee human dignity and, consequently, rights. Yet there is an inherent problem in this stipulation, in Hannah's view: humankind can suddenly, in the spirit of democracy, decide to eliminate an entire people. Relying on the goodwill or assumed goodness of others is a hazardous approach.

On the whole, "the right to have rights," as Hannah characterized the stateless person's situation, is little to rejoice over. Indeed, as contemporary Turkish American philosopher Seyla Benhabib writes, "the 'right to have rights' has become the well-known phrase through which to capture the plight of the stateless, the refugee, the asylum seeker, and the displaced person, that is, the plight of those who have been cast out of the framework 'where one is judged by one's actions and opinions.'" In order for one's rights to be upheld, a person needs a context—a country, a state, or a citizenship that provides them with the necessary sense of belonging. After all, what is a right worth if no one is obliged to uphold it? If everyone—the whole world—carries equal responsibility for upholding these rights, there is a real risk that no one will actually shoulder the burden of making sure they are defended.

The United Nations made its Universal Declaration of Human Rights in 1948, in an attempt to create a set of universal morals that recognized and protected the rights of all human beings. Hannah was deeply critical

of the move, and argued that universal human rights and specific rights based on citizenship are in a complex, contradictory relationship to one another.

She developed her thoughts on the relationship between rights and nation states in *The Origins of Totalitarianism*, writing:

> The Rights of Man, after all, had been defined as "inalienable" because they were supposed to be independent of all governments; but it turned out that the moment human beings lacked their own government and had to fall back upon their minimum rights, no authority was left to protect them and no institution was willing to guarantee them.

Against the backdrop of the forcible divestment of rights from the Jewish people during the 1930s and '40s, Hannah had realized that human rights cannot, in practice, be realized outside of the nation state. When a person is robbed of their citizenship, they are invariably left outside the law; those who have greatest need of state protection—the stateless and refugees—will not have their rights upheld, while those whose citizenship guarantees them formal belonging to a state are not at risk of having their fundamental rights denied. There is without doubt a tension between the ideal that says "all human beings are born free and equal in dignity and rights" and the fact that we can only realize equality within a limited

political community—the context in which a person is judged by their actions and opinions, as Hannah puts it. In her essay "The Rights of Man: What Are They?," Hannah writes that citizenship is the key condition for ensuring that human rights are upheld.

Hannah wrote "The Rights of Man" in 1949, just four years after the end of the war, in the midst of an ongoing refugee crisis. "The world found nothing sacred in the abstract nakedness of being human," she concluded trenchantly. In the essay, she formulates the argument that, to date, human rights have only been realized in the form of citizens' rights. Invoking one's rights does not work if one does not have a state to place demands on, and therefore the right to have rights should be reformulated as the right to have citizenship.

Hannah argues that a state's inbuilt selfishness means that people have a greater chance of seeing their rights championed if they turn to their own government than to some abstract international organization. Despite their dubious qualifications and failures, states and states alone have the ability to offer their citizens comprehensive, constitutional protections that can actually be upheld.

The fundamental principle behind the movement that led to the UN's convention on human rights was based on the idea that all people have a common nature, common needs, and common aspirations, regardless of ethnicity, gender, religion, or nationality. Hannah argues that the refugees and survivors of the concentration camps

revealed that "the abstract nakedness of being human and nothing but human" was actually their greatest threat.

The Holocaust taught us that being deemed human is not enough to protect us from cruelty. Only citizenship can vouchsafe our humanity.

Eighteen

The Holocaust

"YOU KNOW, WHAT WAS DECISIVE was not the year 1933, at least not for me. What was decisive was the day we learned about Auschwitz," Hannah told Günter Gaus in 1964.

In late fall 1942, terrible reports of camps built to annihilate Jews had begun to appear in the American press. Hannah and Heinrich initially struggled to take in the news — "at first, we didn't believe it," Hannah went on, "because militarily it was unnecessary and uncalled for."

Heinrich in particular was skeptical: What possible reason could there be for building death camps? What did the Germans stand to gain? "He said don't be gullible, don't take these stories at face value. They can't go that far!" Hannah explained. And yet, just six months later, the couple were convinced, forced to accept that the

Nazis were capable of far greater atrocities than they could have ever imagined.

Aufbau, the journal Hannah wrote for regularly, was among the first publications to report on the incomprehensible cruelty that went on in the Nazi concentration camps. On December 18, 1942, it published a list of those who had been deported from Camp Gurs to the concentration camps: page after page of names, all belonging to people who had likely been sent to their deaths. Hannah's name could have easily appeared on this list, but she was one of the lucky few who had managed to escape. Little by little, it began to dawn on Hannah that the Nazis had been in the process of solving the "Jewish problem" once and for all.

The Holocaust was unimaginable, "something completely different," in Hannah's words; something that "ought not to have happened." In 1943, when she first learned about Auschwitz, only a fraction of the atrocities that had taken place there were public knowledge, but Hannah later went on to describe Auschwitz as "an industry," a place that produced bodies. The gas chambers, with their adjoining crematoria, were capable of murdering several thousand people at a time.

Most of us now know exactly what went on there. First, the prisoners were led into a changing room under the pretence of being provided showers and disinfection. They then undressed and were ushered into what looked like a large shower room, but was in fact a gas chamber.

Lethal Zyklon B gas, originally intended for delousing, was released from the ceiling, and the people in the gas chamber masquerading as a shower room suffocated. Their dead bodies were dragged out by other prisoners, and taken to an elevator that transported them to the crematorium on the ground level.

The whole process was incredibly efficient, and the brains behind this slick killing machine was a man called Reinhard Heydrich, head of the Reich's security services. On July 31, 1941, when Hermann Göring, head of the German armed forces, issued a written assignment to the SS to prepare "a final solution to the Jewish question," Heydrich was put in charge of organizing the operation. This unleashed a period of frantic strategizing with the ultimate aim of eliminating Jews from a Nazi-controlled Europe. The Final Solution constituted the genocide of the Jewish people—a complete physical annihilation.

Heydrich had been entertaining plans to eradicate the Jewish population for years, and he had considered several different approaches. One early idea was to deport every Jew to the French colony of Madagascar, the so-called Madagascar Plan—but various logistical issues, including the ongoing naval war between Germany and the United Kingdom, meant that particular idea was never put into practice. Deportation to Siberia was also considered, but Heydrich ultimately concluded that the best approach would simply be execution—a neat, cost-effective solution.

In practical terms, however, executing such a large number of people proved unexpectedly difficult. There were over 9 million Jews living in Europe in 1939. Poland alone — which was, of course, occupied by the Germans — was home to 3.3 million Jews, Russia another 3.2 million. Germany still had around 250,000 Jewish inhabitants at the time, and France a further 350,000, roughly half of whom were French citizens. Belgium, the Netherlands, Greece, Norway, and Denmark were also home to many Jews.

Shooting hundreds of thousands of people would take far too long and use far too much ammunition. Heydrich also worried about the psychological impact on the soldiers tasked with murdering so many men, women, and children. Past experience had taught him that few people were capable of systematically executing others without suffering anxiety — and in some cases, having a complete mental breakdown.

As a result, Heydrich found he had no choice but to find a way to kill the Jews other than sending them to the firing squad. Gas had been used previously by the Nazis, during the so-called Aktion T4 program, which saw mentally ill and disabled patients murdered at euthanasia centres.

The systematic execution of those with disabilities — "worthless lives," as they were known to the Nazis — began in 1939, and was initially done by lethal injection, though that particular method was deemed too time-consuming

and long-winded. On the advice of an expert from the National Criminal Police, the Germans decided to try an alternative method of execution. The expert in question proposed carbon monoxide poisoning, which proved to work exceptionally well. Heydrich took this knowledge into account while planning his Final Solution.

By January 1942, Heydrich was ready to present his proposal, and he called a conference in Wannsee, a suburb of Berlin. There were fifteen participants at the ninety-minute meeting, held at a villa owned by the SS. Heydrich led the meeting, and SS-Obersturmbannführer Adolf Eichmann, a senior officer, kept the minutes. A list of Europe's Jewish populations, prepared by Eichmann, was introduced, and Heydrich shared his plans for exterminating the Jewish people: Jews would be assigned to hard physical labour in the east—working on extensive road projects in Georgia and Ukraine, for example. He calculated that a large number of Jews would simply perish from exhaustion. They would, to put it bluntly, work themselves to death. Any Jews unsuited to such work would be sent to concentration camps to be killed.

Heydrich spoke for around an hour, followed by thirty minutes of questions and discussion. Toward the end of the meeting, the various execution methods were debated. Eichmann and Heinrich Müller, the SS-Gruppenführer, explained the advantages of gassing, the method used in the euthanasia program. According to Eichmann's testimony during his trial in Jerusalem in

1961, Heydrich was extremely satisfied once the confer-
ence was over, relaxing in front of the villa's open fire.

The process of dehumanization that began in 1933 with
Gleichschaltung, anti-Jewish laws, anti-Jewish propaganda,
and discrimination, came to its conclusion in the concen-
tration camps of Sobibór, Treblinka, Belzec, Chelmno,
Majdanek, and Auschwitz-Birkenau. The Jews of Europe
were no longer considered human, had been deprived
of their rights and dignity. Instead, they were a problem
to be dealt with, not dissimilar to weeds in a vegetable
patch. They were to be eradicated.

Majdanek, situated just a few kilometres from the
Polish town of Lublin, was the first major concentration
camp to liberated. It is estimated that around 150,000 pris-
oners were brought to the camp between 1942 and 1944.
Of that number, 78,000 were either executed or died of
starvation or typhus. In July 1944, the surviving prisoners
were liberated by the Red Army. On January 27, 1945, the
Soviet troops reached Auschwitz-Birkenau, near Kraków.
The USSR's Red Army had expected fierce resistance, but
instead found that the Germans had already retreated.
Before they abandoned the huge death camp, which was
surrounded by barbed wire, they had blown up the gas
chambers and crematoria. The extensive archive was
destroyed, and 60,000 prisoners had been forced onto a
death march toward the camps in Germany.

Hundreds of bodies that the Germans had not
managed to burn were left in the camp, along with

around 7,000 prisoners who were either too sick or too weak to leave. No one who has seen the images from the liberation of Auschwitz will ever be able to forget them: the children in oversized striped uniforms behind the barbed-wire fences; the piles of shoes that belonged to the dead; the emaciated men and women whose eyes seem much too large.

Following the liberation of Auschwitz-Birkenau, the remaining concentration and death camps were all liberated. Despite the Germans' best efforts to destroy all evidence, there was ample proof of their atrocities, of the terrible crimes they had committed. The soldiers involved in freeing the camps spoke of mountains of false teeth, eyeglasses, and wedding rings. Several tonnes of women's hair was found, along with hundreds of thousands of shoes, piles of clothing and suitcases, watches, and gold teeth. The soldiers found mass graves and dead bodies stacked one on top of another. Then there were the people — the starving, terrified people who had survived: the men, women, and children.

The Allied forces had known what was going on in the German camps since 1942, but no one could have imagined the extent of the operation. The images, films, and testimonies from the camps shocked the world. The evil that took place there was incomprehensible, the systematic cruelty unimaginable. The whole world demanded to know how such a thing could have occurred.

Countless books have since been written about the Holocaust, with philosophers, psychologists, sociologists, and historians all attempting to answer the question of how the unthinkable became reality. How could it have happened? In 1946, the Nazis being held prisoner in Nuremberg, Germany, were subjected to extensive psychological evaluations involving interviews, observation, intelligence tests, handwriting analysis, and Rorschach tests — a kind of personality assessment involving non-figurative images in the form of ink blots.

Thirty years later, Molly Harrower, one of ten Rorschach experts who analyzed the material from Nuremberg, wrote that there was nothing remarkable to be found. There was simply no evidence of the unique psychopathology, or "Nazi personality," that the general public were expecting. Rudolf Hess, Hitler's deputy, displayed a number of grandiose and bizarre traits, and Joachim von Ribbentrop, the foreign minister, was possibly depressed, but none of the experts were willing to draw any broader conclusions, said Harrower, primarily because of the lack of any striking findings.

The world clamoured for an explanation for the inexplicable. But beyond that, there was perhaps an even greater need to demonize those involved. The demonization of criminals is one way of processing incomprehensible cruelty, by enabling distance. During the 1960s, a number of books seeking to describe the so-called Nazi personality were published, despite the fact

that there was no empirical evidence of any such thing. The archetypal Nazi was described either as a lonely, failed individual with a lack of self-confidence, or as a hyper-intelligent psychopath with sadistic tendencies.

Eventually, Hannah's contemporaries Theodor Adorno, Max Horkheimer, Norbert Elias, and Erich Fromm gave the people what the experts at Nuremberg had been unable to. Adorno and Horkheimer claimed that Nazism derived from an "authoritarian personality" that could not handle the complexity and diversity of modern life. Norbert Elias described "a new type of person" who shifted the boundaries of shame and replaced social compulsions with psychological ones. In *Escape from Freedom*, Fromm argued that the freedoms enjoyed by modern humans produced anxiety, leading to a willingness to subordinate oneself to fascist ideologies.

Then, of course, there was Hannah Arendt. Inspired by political scientist Raul Hilberg's study titled *The Destruction of the European Jews*, she wrote in *The Origins of Totalitarianism* that the Nazi criminals were a product of a totalitarian system, a regime that controls and dominates all aspects of life. Is that a sufficient explanation? Hannah was not done with the question, and when Adolf Eichmann was arrested and put on trial in Jerusalem, charged with genocide and crimes against humanity, she saw a chance to further examine the Nazi personality and try to understand the motives that a man like Eichmann may have had.

Nineteen

The Banality of Evil

HANNAH AND HEINRICH SPENT the summer of 1960 in a charming, Swiss-style guest house in the Catskills, a mountainous region in southeastern New York State. They had travelled down there with a group of close friends, many of them Europeans in exile, and Hannah spent her days reading and writing, and her nights socializing. They ate dinner, played chess, and swam in the pool. As evening approached, they would go out to drink at one of the local bars.

Life was good. After close to twenty years in the United States, Hannah and Heinrich were settled in what had become their homeland. They had moved from their first cramped apartment to a larger place on Riverside Drive, and Hannah, who had barely spoken a word of English when the SS *Guiné* docked in New York in May 1941, had published several books in English—among

them *The Origins of Totalitarianism*, which transformed her into a global intellectual celebrity. Both Hannah and Heinrich had begun teaching college students and were part of a larger group of intellectual New Yorkers.

In Hannah and Heinrich's spacious apartment, not far from Central Park, they often hosted friends for dinner. The discussions were lively and engaged, sometimes loud, and there was frequent laughter. Together, the couple had managed to create a life that was theirs—a home, a place in the world. The horrors of the Second World War felt a long way away.

That summer of 1960, however, memories of the war came flooding back. Adolf Eichmann had been arrested by Israeli agents in Argentina, where he had managed to hide away for almost as long as Hannah and Heinrich had been in the United States. Eichmann and his wife, Veronica, had created a simple life for themselves in Buenos Aires, together with their four sons, and the newspapers were full of reports on his arrest. Speculation was rife, and the news became a natural topic of conversation among the group of friends in the Catskills. One of the questions being mulled over by the press was the location of his trial—everyone agreed that Eichmann should face justice, but where? Should the trial be held in Argentina or Israel?

Hannah began toying with the idea of attending the trial, discussing the subject with Karl Jaspers in a number of letters. Eventually, she decided to leave it to

fate: she would attend the trial if it was held in Israel. And so it was.

On her return from the Catskills, Hannah got in touch with William Shawn, editor of the *New Yorker*, and made him an offer: she could cover the trial for the magazine the following spring. Naturally, Shawn agreed. Hannah was a respected, celebrated intellectual voice in the U.S., and she also had her own painful experiences of the Nazi atrocities in Europe, of anti-Semitism and persecution. It is hard to think of anyone better placed to follow and report on the trial against one of the Nazis' worst criminals.

On April 7, 1961, Hannah flew to Tel Aviv and then made her way to Jerusalem. She wrote to Heinrich, back home in New York, that Jerusalem was cold but sunny. Several of Hannah's friends had settled in Israel, and while she waited for the trial to begin, she spent some time with the Klenbort and Blumenfeld families.

The trial of Adolf Eichmann was the first to be broadcast on television, and Israel's prime minister, David Ben-Gurion, had high expectations: he saw the public trial as a history lesson of sorts, and hoped it would help the young Jews in Israel, with no first-hand experience of European anti-Semitism, to understand the full extent of the Holocaust. It would also serve as a powerful reminder of the Jews' fate to the wider world.

Hannah Arendt was not the only celebrity present for the trial. Jerusalem was teeming with renowned figures,

with intellectuals, writers, and journalists who wanted to
see Eichmann — "the monster from Linz" — with their
own eyes. Big names like the philosopher and mathem-
atician Bertrand Russell and the writer and Holocaust
survivor Elie Wiesel were among the spectators. The
American television company Capital Cities had been
given access to Beit Ha'am, the building in which the
trial would take place, and planned to broadcast to the
world. In the end, a total of forty countries went on to
broadcast *The State of Israel v. Adolf Eichmann.*

When the trial began, however, it proved something
of a disappointment. Hannah sent a letter to Heinrich,
describing it as a big, macabre performance. On April
20, 1961, she wrote: "The whole thing so damned banal
and indescribably low and repulsive." Hannah was angry,
and felt that the trial was nothing but a shameful spec-
tacle. Her tone is sarcastic, and the same mood resonates
through the book she wrote about the trial, *Eichmann in
Jerusalem: A Report on the Banality of Evil.*

The accused, Adolf Eichmann, spent the entire trial
sitting calmly in a bulletproof glass box. He had a bad
cold, and kept blowing his nose throughout. He was also,
as Hannah told Heinrich, unbearably dull to listen to.
Dry, pale, and proper — almost a caricature of the laced-
up bureaucrat. That is how Hannah went on to describe
Eichmann in her book: as a dull official who was just
doing his job.

Hannah presented Eichmann the same way in her

series of articles for the *New Yorker*: as an unimaginative bureaucrat who was simply obeying orders. Her argument caused a fierce debate, to say the least, and many were angered by her depiction of the Nazi war criminal. Hannah's description of Eichmann went against the picture of him that had been cultivated so far, as someone evil and demonic. Her laconic representation was seen as apologetic, and her honest reports were interpreted as a defence of Eichmann. A short passage criticizing the occupied countries' Jewish councils' willingness to co-operate with the SS during the war—Hannah argued that some of them had actually collaborated with the Nazis—was also seen as an attempt to place blame on the Jewish people:

> In Amsterdam as in Warsaw, in Berlin as in Budapest, Jewish officials could be trusted to compile the lists of persons and of their property, to secure money from the deportees to defray the expenses of their deportation and extermination, to keep track of vacated apartments, to supply police forces to help seize Jews and get them on trains, until, as a last gesture, they handed over the assets of the Jewish community in good order for final confiscation. They distributed Yellow Star badges, and sometimes, as in Warsaw, "the sale of the armbands became a regular business; there were ordinary armbands of cloth and fancy plastic armbands which were washable."

Perhaps, Hannah suggested, fewer Jews would have died if the Jewish leaders had been less willing to collaborate.

This argument was, of course, misinterpreted: many seemed unable to distinguish between the concepts of responsibility and guilt. To be accountable, shouldering some of the responsibility, is not the same as being guilty. But the mistaken notion that Hannah was blaming the Jewish people for their own persecution, for the Holocaust, quickly took hold, and Hannah was forced to put up with questions about why she thought the Jews were responsible for their own deaths, in virtually every interview until she herself died.

Following the publication of *Eichmann in Jerusalem*, Hannah was repeatedly described as heartless and devoid of empathy, accused of being cold and indifferent. Colleagues turned their backs on her, and friends cut off contact with her. Kurt Blumenfeld would never forgive her, and Hans Jonas, one of her closest friends since her university days in Germany, was dismayed, refusing to speak to Hannah for over a year. Siegfried Moses, an old acquaintance from Berlin, publicly declared war on Hannah, and her friend Gershom Scholem lamented that Hannah did not love the Jewish people — only the Jews she happened to be friends with. The media described Hannah as anti-Zionist, a self-hating Jew, and anti-Israel. She was accused of betraying the Jewish people. Over the weeks, months, and years that followed, hundreds of hateful letters arrived in her mailbox.

SO WHAT HAD SHE MEANT? What was it Hannah wished to convey? Today, her concept of "the banality of evil" is well known and uncontroversial. In *Eichmann in Jerusalem*, she questions the idea that evil deeds imply evil intentions and evil motives, writing that there is not always a relationship between the three. Hannah's statement should not be understood as an attempt to trivialize or deny evil. Rather, she posits that it is not the evil itself that is banal, but the motives behind the evil deed.

It seems, however, that the Jewish intellectuals who criticized *Eichmann in Jerusalem* were more upset by Hannah's criticism of the Jewish councils than her descriptions of Eichmann; to claim that the Jewish people bore any responsibility whatsoever for the Holocaust was highly controversial. The Jewish councils, or *Judenräte* as they were referred to by the Nazi regime, were administrative bodies that all Jewish communities across the occupied territories were required to form, to serve as intermediaries between the communities and the regime. In this context, these councils were distinct from the forms of self-government that Jewish communities had themselves established in previous centuries. Looking back after the event — at the incredibly negative reactions to her criticism of the Jewish councils — Hannah realized that she should have been clearer in her arguments about their behaviour during the war. Ahead of an interview with *Look* magazine in September 1963, she jotted down the following notes in

response to the case that had been made in defence of the Jewish councils:

1. "Better, if you have to die, to be selected by your kin." — I disagree: it would have been infinitely better to let the Nazis do their own murderous business.

2. "With a 100 victims we shall save a 1,000." — This sounds to me like the last version of human sacrifices: pick seven virgins, sacrifice them to placate the wrath of the gods. Well, this is not my religious belief, and [it] most certainly is not the faith of Judaism.

3. Finally, the theory of the lesser evil. Result: good men do the worst.

The points above are implicit in Hannah's reasoning in the book on Eichmann, but were obviously not elaborated clearly enough. In essence, her criticism boils down to responsibility: what responsibility did the Jewish councils take for their community members when they willingly supplied the Nazi regime with lists of addresses, enabling the SS to easily, effortlessly, round up Jews for onward transport to concentration camps? Of course, we must remember a particular factor when we engage in any discussion of the Jewish councils' responsibility

for their situation: the fact that they were, undoubt-
edly, victims too. Members of the Jewish councils were
exposed, and they feared persecution for good reason.
What demands can we really place on such victims?
What can we ask of people living under threat, in acute
danger, fully aware of the cruelty awaiting them? Is it not
immoral—inhumane and heartless, even—to blame the
victims, as Hannah did?

One of the few people to actually defend Hannah's
book on Eichmann, and her discussion of the Jewish
councils and their responsibility, was Bruno Bettelheim.
Bettelheim was born in Vienna in 1903, and, like Hannah,
grew up in a secular Jewish home. In May 1938, shortly
after the Nazis invaded Austria, Bettelheim was sent
first to Dachau and then to Buchenwald. In a stroke of
almost unbelievable luck, he managed to survive two of
the most notorious concentration camps: in late April
1939 he was released, along with several hundred others,
in an amnesty in honour of Adolf Hitler's birthday.

Bettelheim drew on his own experiences of the concen-
tration camps when he wrote about the Holocaust, and
like Hannah, he argued that the Jews in Europe bore a
certain amount of responsibility for what had happened.
He wrote a positive review of *Eichmann in Jerusalem* for
the *New Republic*, and developed his thoughts in *Surviving
and Other Essays*, among other places. Bettelheim goes
further than Hannah in his criticism, singling out the
individuals and groups (such as the Jewish councils)

who did not do all they could to make things harder for the Germans. It may have been possible to save lives, he argues, through sabotage, resistance, or other deeds that hindered or undermined German power.

Bruno Bettelheim refused to regard the Jews as entirely blameless. He states that to do so would mean remembering them as less than human, as beings without their own free will or intelligence. While they lived, he writes, they had responsibilities and duties, and to deny that, or to ignore their mistakes, would be unjust both to them and to those who showed bravery. Bettelheim argues that every person has a responsibility, but that in the end it is, of course, not the victims who should assume any guilt, but their executioners.

Judith Nisse Shklar, a philosopher of Jewish heritage, built on Bruno Bettelheim's arguments in her book *Ordinary Vices*. Shklar was born in Latvia in 1928 and was forced to flee with her parents as a result of the war, first to Japan and later to the United States and finally Canada. Like both Hannah and Bettelheim, she had a deep, personal understanding of the Holocaust. Throughout her professional life, she was interested in the concept of cruelty, and she discusses Bruno Bettelheim's ideas of victims and responsibility in relation to that concept.

Shklar begins with the notion that the victims of the Holocaust were ordinary people who were subjected to extraordinary cruelty. They were neither saints nor heroes, and she argues that idealizing the victims is just

as harmful as blaming them. Shklar views both reactions as an expression of our inability to confront cruelty.

Shklar's argument can help us understand why Hannah's criticism of the Jewish councils' actions offended so many people. Our idealization of the victims of the Holocaust, of those who were subjected to the unfathomable brutality of the Nazi regime, creates a distance between us, the spectators, and the victims. It is only once we understand that those who died in the Nazi death camps were ordinary people like you and me, with faults and merits, that we can really grasp the scope of the horrors they faced. They were not martyrs, they were not saints or heroes; they were ordinary people in a terrible situation.

Hannah shocked her contemporaries, not simply with her disapproval of the Jewish councils, but also by claiming that Eichmann was neither demonic nor fanatical, neither evil nor malevolent. Eichmann had simply done his job, as efficiently and as well as he could. "Whatever he did he did, as far as he could see, as a law-abiding citizen. He did his *duty*, as he told the police and the court over and over again; he not only obeyed *orders*, he also obeyed the *law*," she writes in *Eichmann in Jerusalem*. She goes on:

> And just as the law in civilized countries assumes that the voice of conscience tells everybody "Thou shalt not kill," even though man's natural desires and

inclinations may at times be murderous, so the law of
Hitler's land demanded that the voice of conscience tell
everybody: "Thou shalt kill," although the organizers
of the massacres knew full well that murder is against
the normal desires and inclinations of most people. Evil
in the Third Reich had lost the quality by which most
people recognize it—the quality of temptation. Many
Germans and many Nazis, probably an overwhelm-
ing majority of them, must have been tempted *not* to
murder, *not* to rob, *not* to let their neighbours go off to
their doom (for that the Jews were transported to their
doom they knew, of course, even though many of them
may not have known the gruesome details), and not to
become accomplices in all these crimes by benefitting
from them. But, God knows, they had learned how to
resist temptation.

In this passage, Hannah is drawing a link to Kant's theory
of evil. Kant takes a concept he calls "radical evil" as
his starting point, an idea that involves allowing our
own desires to overrule our duty to listen to, and act in
accordance with, goodwill. Evil, then, in Kant's view, is
a temptation.

Hannah also talks about evil in those terms, and she
emphasizes the importance of looking at evil itself as
a temptation. Not because evil per se is what we truly
want and need—a cake that, as Nietzsche might have put
it, we would be foolish to deny ourselves—but because

"temptation" implies something forbidden or taboo, and because ideas that are forbidden wake a certain desire in us. In the Third Reich, evil and cruelty were no longer tempting, because cruelty and evil were not forbidden; they were decreed. Eichmann, therefore, had not succumbed to temptation when he sent hundreds of thousands of people to the gas chambers.

Implicit in this is an uncomfortable truth: that people have a tendency to follow the path of least resistance, to ignore their conscience and do what everyone else is doing. As the exclusion, persecution, and, ultimately, annihilation of Jews became normalized, there were few who protested, who stood up for their own principles.

Hannah does not rule out the possibility that a small number of people are genuinely evil by nature. She discusses the Biblical view of evil and points out that not even the Bible speaks of intentional evil. Cain did not *want* to become Cain when he murdered his brother Abel; and Judas—the principal example of human sin—hanged himself once he understood the extent of his betrayal. They did not know what they were doing, and therefore had to be forgiven their sins. Jesus preached forgiveness for all sins that could, in one way or another, be explained away as human weakness—in other words, as a result of the corrupt human nature that, due to original sin, is inclined toward evil. Humans are weak, and they fall easily into temptation. Because this fallibility is understandable, forgiveness is possible.

There is, however, one exception, Hannah writes. Jesus says that there are also those who commit something known in Greek as *skandalon*—acts so immoral and unbearable that it would be better if the guilty party had never been born. Jesus does not elaborate on the nature or content of these evil deeds, but it seems as though he considers them unforgivable, an attitude that Hannah shares: there are evil deeds, and evil people, who can neither be forgiven nor punished. Not all evil can be explained in terms of obedience, ignorance, or neglect. There is such a thing as evil that is as incomprehensible as it is unforgivable.

The issue of evil was not resolved with the invention of the term "the banality of evil." The question remained, and would continue to dominate Hannah's thoughts. The horrors of the concentration camps brought the matter to a head, and there were no philosophical theories or psychological models of explanation that could make them comprehensible. In *The Life of the Mind*, published posthumously in 1978, Hannah writes:

> The concentration camps are the laboratories where changes in human nature are tested...in their effort to prove that everything is possible, totalitarian regimes have discovered without knowing it that there are crimes which man can neither punish nor forgive. When the impossible was made possible it became the unpunishable, unforgivable absolute evil

which could no longer be understood and explained by the evil motives of self-interest, greed, covetousness, resentment, lust for power, and cowardice; and which therefore anger could not revenge, love could not endure, friendship could not forgive.

Hannah continued in her attempts to understand evil until the very end. More recent critics such as American Holocaust researcher Deborah Lipstadt and British historian David Cesarani are not entirely justified when they attack Hannah's theory of the banality of evil for being one-dimensional and incomplete. Hannah never claimed that the theory was comprehensive. She was no stranger to the idea that there may be genuinely evil people out there, people driven by a desire to hurt others. That there must be someone leading the way, someone initiating the evil, someone creating the context, ideology, or prejudices necessary for the obedient masses to blindly adopt.

Twenty

Evil and Responsibility

HOW SHOULD EVIL BE MET or resisted? Hannah believed in responsibility, reflection, and reason, and she lived her life in accordance with those convictions.

If I had to describe Hannah's character in one word, I would say that she was responsible. In every situation, she took responsibility. When Nazism and anti-Semitism began to flourish in Germany during the 1930s, she resisted by becoming involved in the Zionist movement; when she was living in exile in France, she helped Jewish children find sanctuary in Mandatory Palestine; while she was interned in Gurs, she kept up her own and the others' morale, and when the opportunity to escape arose, she tried to convince her fellow internees to escape with her. I could go on—responsibility runs like a common thread through every period of her life, and she demanded no more and no less from others.

Even as a girl, Hannah took responsibility for others. During the summer of 1911, Hannah's father, Paul, was taken ill and institutionalized. The syphilis he had contracted in his youth flared up with full force, and he spent two years in hospital. Young Hannah showed great patience during his illness. Her mother documents the young girl's heartbreaking concern for her dying father in her journal: Hannah spent hours playing cards with Paul, who was bedridden for much of the time, and she prayed for him every morning and night. Two years after her father fell sick, in March 1913, Hannah's beloved grandfather, Max Arendt, died. Paul followed him just seven months later, after a long battle with his illness.

In *Unser Kind*, Martha describes, with some concern, Hannah's reaction to her grandfather and father's deaths:

> In October [1913] Paul dies. She takes that to be something sad for me. She herself remains untouched by it. To console me she says: "Remember, Mama, that it happens to a lot of women." She attends the funeral and weeps [she told me] "because of the beautiful singing." ... She probably derives something like satisfaction from the attentions lavished on her by so many people. — Otherwise she is a sunny, cheerful child with a good heart.

Hannah's mother took her seven-year-old daughter's concern for her as indifference toward the deaths that had

struck the family, but to me, this is a strange interpretation. Instead, it seems obvious that the precocious young girl's forced happiness was a way of taking responsibility. Hannah noticed her mother's grief and worries, and decided to take on the burden of a situation she could not control by putting her own feelings and sorrow to one side. Hannah did not want to trouble her already depressed mother by openly showing her pain, and so she became a source of support instead.

As an adult, Hannah rarely spoke about that time in her life, dominated by the loss of her beloved father and grandfather—perhaps because it was such a painful period? Perhaps because, in taking responsibility for her mother, she did not give herself the opportunity to grieve for either Max or Paul? In the many hundreds of letters Hannah wrote to her friends, she comes across as an extremely empathetic and considerate person, with a strong desire to support others in any way she could.

RESPONSIBILITY IS A RECURRING THEME in Hannah's books. What does it mean to take responsibility? What are we, as humans, responsible for—and for whom are we responsible? Everyone has a range of perceptions about themselves, as well as aspirations for the type of person they want to be. Some of these beliefs and perceptions are more than simple expressions of preference or taste. They have a deeper meaning, something existential

and moral. They express what is often known as an individual's "moral identity." This consists of the norms and values that a person has made their own, whether through active, conscious choices, or through influence, treatment, and upbringing—and which, in various ways, set limits for our behaviour.

Aristotle wrote that an individual's character is shaped by the decisions they make. When choices, actions, and decisions are repeated, they become habits, and gradually express themselves as permanent features of an individual's character. Hannah argues along the same lines in *Responsibility and Judgment*, to name just one source. She writes that one's moral character has nothing to do with either aptitude or intelligence, but reflection; with acting and taking responsibility for one's actions. In Hannah's view, an individual creates their moral worth by a sequence of reflected choices on how to act or not act. The quality of being a person is thus distinguished from merely being human, and the integrity of this personhood is upheld by the coherence of these choices. This argument contains echoes not only of Aristotelian virtue ethics, but existentialism too.

Hannah Arendt was reluctant to call herself a philosopher, yet she built herself a philosophical system around the concept of responsibility and the moral phenomena that can be linked to it—such as guilt, shame, blame, evil, and goodness. In *The Human Condition* and *Responsibility and Judgment* in particular, Hannah

developed a philosophical approach that held at its very heart the capacity of humankind to bear responsibility. Despite her experiences to the contrary, Hannah had an unshakable belief in the ability of people to make their own independent, rational decisions; since humans are free, they are also responsible.

Hannah's life experiences had given her a deep understanding of the importance of personal responsibility. While she came across as strict to some, she was never stricter on anyone than she was on herself. This austerity, combined with a great passion for the truth, meant she was occasionally misunderstood. The controversy surrounding her book on Eichmann is a clear example of this effect. Hannah, who always did her utmost to understand what others meant, was not prepared for the hostile reception of *Eichmann in Jerusalem*. "The criticism is directed at an 'image,' and this image has been substituted for the book I wrote," she dejectedly told her friend Mary McCarthy in October 1963.

The hounding that began after the publication of her writing on Eichmann, the anger and ill will that reared its ugly head, shook Hannah to her core. "And what surprises and shocks me most of all," she wrote to Mary in late fall 1963, "is the tremendous amount of hatred and hostility lying around and waiting only for a chance to break out."

Hannah's genuine surprise at the animosity directed toward her is moving, because it is evidence of her

fundamentally positive view of humankind. She saw the best in people, and thus she was despairing and surprised when they let her down.

Twenty-One

On Love and Fidelity

"LOVE," WRITES HANNAH ARENDT in *The Human Condition*, is "one of the rarest occurrences in human lives." The claim will surprise anyone with more than a passing knowledge of Hannah's story. Men and love affairs seemed to follow one after another throughout her life; there were times when she was involved with two men at once, and one of Hannah's friends described her as "something of a femme fatale." She was a very popular woman, someone who found herself the centre of attention no matter the company she was in.

Given that love does not seem to have been a rare occurrence in Hannah's life, what did she mean there? The answer comes in a footnote to the above quote:

The common prejudice that love is as common as "romance" may be due to the fact that we all learned

about it first through poetry. But the poets fool us; they
are the only ones to whom love is not only a crucial,
but an indispensable experience, which entitles them
to mistake it for a universal one.

Hannah was in her fifties when she made this sober,
possibly even disillusioned distinction between love and
romance. She was writing with the experience of a grown
woman, and with many years' reflection on the concept
of love under her belt.

Love is not simply a psychological phenomenon, but a
philosophical notion that has been subject to considera-
tion and analysis for thousands of years. Plato's dialogues,
for example, discuss two contradictory theories of love.
Love can, in the first instance, be seen as a being's desire
to be reunited with its missing half, a longing to be
whole again, to merge together to form a single unit.
The second definition of love provided by Plato is more
to do with desire than fusion. In this, the essence of love
is desire for an object, for *the other.*

Hannah's exposition of the nature of love in *The
Human Condition* is similar to the concept of love as a
union, which is, itself, a development of Plato's vision of
love as fusion. Seen from this angle, love consists of the
creation of a "we" — a single unit.

British philosopher Roger Scruton is one of those
who adheres to this view. In *Sexual Desire: A Philosophical
Investigation,* he writes that love is present "just so soon

as all distinction between my interests and your inter-
ests is overcome." Love makes the two become one, an
indivisible unit, each party as dependent as the other,
and each equally engaged in the other's prosperity. In
love there is, as Scruton writes, no difference between
my interests and yours. Or, as Hannah puts it, there is no
longer anything "in-between" the two people. The only
thing that can come between two lovers, Hannah goes
on, is a child, "love's own product."

Those in love turn their backs on their surround-
ings; they become a "we" that no longer needs the
outside world. Their love makes them strangers, or
perhaps indifferent, to the world and worldly things.
What does someone in love care about the news, the
bills, the weather? In the world of lovers, there is only
their love, and that is enough. Enough to turn the entire
world upside down. But if love is, by its very nature,
"unworldly," making the two lovers strangers to every-
thing around them, then a child, the product of their
love, is what reconnects them to the world: "Through
the child, it is as though the lovers return to the world
from which their love had expelled them."

The birth of a child, with all its concrete and rather
prosaic needs, brings them back to the material realm.
A child cannot live on love alone; it needs worldly things
like food and clean diapers, order, and routine. This is
why a child also represents the end of love: "This new
worldliness, the possible result and the only possible

happy ending of a love affair, is, in a sense, the end of love, which must either overcome the partners anew or be transformed into another mode of belonging together."

Love matures into another type of union when a child enters a loving couple's lives, demanding a place in their unit. The child forces the lovers to leave their intoxicated state and return to the real world, to everyday life: a beautiful description of parenthood.

Hannah and Heinrich never had any children of their own. "When we were young enough to have children, we had no money, and when we had money, we were too old," Hannah told her friend, the philosopher Hans Jonas. Heinrich had another explanation: "We decided not to have children in times such as these. We are sad about it, but a sense of responsibility for those who might be innocent sufferers is a valuable thing," he wrote to his mother, Klara Blücher, in April 1946.

Despite Hannah's theory that a child is the only "happy ending" of a love affair, Hannah and Heinrich's love survived without. What transformed their love into something more than an affair, into what Hannah describes as "another mode of belonging together," was their shared passion for thinking. Hannah dedicated *The Origins of Totalitarianism* to Heinrich, and referred to it as "our book." The dialogue they established in the spring of 1936 never petered out. They continued to talk, to ask questions, to wonder, and to challenge each other.

When Hannah first met Heinrich, she had struggled

with her anxiety. In a letter sent from Geneva, dated September 18, 1937, she describes her worries of being erased in a love affair, of losing her independence, her freedom, herself:

> You see, dearest, I always knew, even as a kid, that I can only truly exist in love. And that is why I was so frightened that I might simply get lost. And so I made myself independent. And about the love of others who branded me as cold-hearted, I always thought: if you only knew how dangerous love would be for me.

What was she so afraid of? There is an inherent risk to the type of love Hannah describes in her letter: love as a merging of two individuals with differing interests risks erasing one and allowing the other to dominate. To metaphorically merge with another person and form a new whole is a romantic thought, but also a terrifying one. A happy union presupposes two equally strong individuals, who, in the deepest sense of the word, are actually able to think of the other's interests and desires as being as important as their own.

Is it possible to live with another person without disappearing yourself? How does one avoid being drawn into the other's life to such an extent that one's own self is erased? That is one of the key issues philosopher Emmanuel Levinas examines in his work. Like Hannah, Levinas was forced to flee Germany, and he too chose

France, where he lived in exile until his death. Levinas was faithful to the Husserlian phenomenology he had studied in Freiburg, and devoted his life to an understanding of ethics based on experienced phenomena.

The basis of ethics, according to Levinas, is in an encounter with "the other"; it is only when we really see the other that the conception of ethics awakes. In this approach it is important to see the other as *another*, as a "You" to relate to. Love, then, must necessarily give space to two individuals.

The happy union assumes, paradoxically, that the coupling of two people allows space for both to continue to be themselves. This is precisely what Hannah and Heinrich seem to have managed — being dependent on each other without smothering each other; merging together without being erased; continuing to be two individuals within their union. Is that not vital to a relationship — that it consists of two identifiable, distinct parties? Otherwise, if the two really do become one, what is there left to love?

Heinrich Blücher had been married twice and had already experienced countless relationships when he met Hannah. She embodied something he had never encountered before, or perhaps had not been mature enough to notice earlier. As a young man, he had always sought out intellectual equals among men. His discussions were with men, not women; he listened to men, and he read men. But when he met Hannah, his prejudices were

turned on their head. She was, without doubt, his true intellectual equal, and she was also more educated and disciplined than he was.

In meeting Hannah, which involved romance, eroticism, and intellectual exchange, he was forced to reassess his views of women, leading him to assert in a lecture at Bard College in 1952 that equality between a man and a woman was the very basis of a functioning marriage.

Equality should not, however, be mistaken for similarity. Both Hannah and Heinrich seem to have had relatively conservative views on gender and on what is considered masculine or feminine. "I always thought that there are certain occupations that are improper for women, that do not become them, if I may put it that way. It just doesn't look good when a woman gives orders. She should try not to get into such a situation if she wants to remain feminine," Hannah said of women's liberation.

Despite being relatively progressive, Hannah and Heinrich's marriage was not without its problems. The affair Heinrich began with a young Russian Jew in 1948, for example, while Hannah was in New Hampshire for two months, put their love, and perhaps above all Hannah's faith in Heinrich, to the test. Heinrich had not promised Hannah anything more than to be faithful in his own way, meaning emotionally and intellectually — but not necessarily sexually. Hannah struggled to accept

his definition of fidelity, and she was incredibly upset when Heinrich's affair became common knowledge among their friends.

And yet, Hannah made a real effort to handle the whole situation with composure; she prided herself on her Berliner attitudes regarding love, sexuality, and fidelity. In her essay on Bertolt Brecht, she describes the Berliner approach as follows: "To be sure, in this world there is no eternal love, or even ordinary faithfulness. There is nothing but the intensity of the moment; that is, passion, which is even a bit more perishable than man himself." In accordance with this *Liebe berliner Art* (love in a Berlin fashion), she viewed marital loyalty as superior to sexual fidelity.

Brecht's attitude — described here by Hannah — expresses the same carefree approach in relation to love that she found in the poetry of Robert Gilbert, Heinrich's collaborator in Berlin. The message of both was to not take anything too seriously; life is short, so why not make the most of any love and happiness we get?

Hannah and Heinrich were likely both influenced by the anarchist spirit that was *à la mode* in relationships in Paris and Berlin in the interwar years. Brecht praised fleeting passion and rejected ideas of eternal love and fidelity, and in 1920s Paris, the Surrealists argued for free love. André Breton's 1924 Surrealist manifesto, *Manifeste du surréalisme*, argued for the liberation of the individual and the reshaping of society. The liberated

individual, of course, practised free love and believed in open relationships.

Jean-Paul Sartre and Simone de Beauvoir lived in an open relationship guided by these very principles. Their pact giving one another permission to indulge in extra-marital sexual relations without these having any impact on their own relationship was well known, and in theory, it seems to have worked incredibly well. On a purely rational level, one may conclude that a person cannot own another's body, and that it is both unreasonable and immoral to demand sexual exclusivity from another. The key to a loving relationship is not sexual fidelity but intellectual communion, loyalty, and emotional exclusivity — you can sleep with as many people as you like, but you can only give your heart to one person. That is the argument, and it sounds both sensible and reasonable, intellectually honourable and well thought through — but how does it work in reality?

Well, perhaps not quite so well as in theory. Simone's meeting with fellow author Nelson Algren turned her intellectual relationship with Sartre on its head. In fact, she eventually found herself on the verge of leaving Sartre for Algren, the man she described as the love of her life. De Beauvoir chronicled this love triangle — and her anguish — in her novel *The Mandarins* (awarded the Prix Goncourt in 1954). Her debut novel, *She Came to Stay*, depicts another love triangle: intellectuals Françoise and Pierre are in a loving yet open relationship, and they invite

a rootless young woman into their lives. Pierre becomes infatuated, if not obsessed, by the young Xavière, and Françoise struggles with her feelings of jealousy. It is impossible not to read the novel as a fictionalization of de Beauvoir's own struggle to accept her lover's erotic escapades with others.

Dora and Bertrand Russell seem to have had a similar experience, suggesting that what appears reasonable and right in theory can prove much more complex in practice. In *The Right to Be Happy*, published in 1927, Dora Russell— whose husband was considerably older and more famous than her—criticizes the seemingly straightforward link between possession and love. She was convinced that we need freedom in order to be happy, and thus found the notion of monogamy reprehensible. Dora argued that a couple cannot make each other happy by owning each other, each other's bodies, or each other's sexuality. She therefore urged everyone, men and women alike, to liberate themselves from the limitations that society, religion, and convention try to place on them.

Dora Russell was likely influenced by the Bloomsbury Group's attitudes to sexuality, love, and fidelity. The Bloomsbury Group was made up of intellectuals, writers, and artists such as E. M. Forster, Virginia Woolf, and Vita Sackville-West, and was active primarily during the interwar years. The group was based in Bloomsbury, London, and several of its members had studied at Trinity College, Cambridge. They rebelled

against Victorian values and, like the Surrealists in Paris, practised free love.

Even Bertrand Russell, Dora's husband, wrote a book on the theme of love, sexuality, and marriage. In *Marriage and Morals*, published a couple of years after Dora's appeal for free love, he repeats her theories and arguments. We cannot own one another, Bertrand claims; human beings are by nature free, even as sexual beings. In theory, the couple were very much in agreement and had almost certainly spent many hours discussing issues like fidelity, love, sex, and freedom. And yet they divorced in 1935. The extramarital affairs they had both engaged in destroyed their relationship.

Not even Hannah was as true to her Berlin values in practice as she was in theory, and she struggled with Heinrich's stance on fidelity. To him, flirting or even having sex with someone else was not a big deal, but to Hannah it was a betrayal, something that several entries in her *Denktagebuch,* her intellectual diary, bear witness to. It is heartbreaking to read her attempts to rational-ize events that have had a deep emotional impact on her, and yet her rationalizing also says so much about Hannah as a person: she faced up to the difficulties in her life with her intellect. She tried to establish control over both political unease and personal emotional chaos by analyzing, discussing, and defining. As though both internal and external disorder could be filed away in neat, philosophical categories.

In 1950, Hannah wrote a longer reflection on the theme of fidelity in her *Denktagebuch*. She distinguishes between two types of infidelity: the "more or less inno-cent infidelity" that has to do with life itself, present in our very life force; and "the great crime of infidelity" that "murders that which was true ... that which one brought into the world."

She writes that infidelity is

> true destruction because it is only through fidelity that we have any sway over our past: fidelity's existence depends on us. If the possibility of truth and that which is true did not exist, fidelity would be nothing more than a synonym of stubbornness. If fidelity did not exist, the truth would have no substance and would, therefore, be utterly meaningless.

In the reflection above, Hannah links fidelity to truth and meaning, to the very foundation of existence. In other words, she placed great importance on fidelity, but made the "more or less innocent infidelity" — an expression of "vitality" that includes sexual affairs and flirting — banal. The zest of life, *joie de vivre*, can lead to infidelity, but that would make it an innocent infidelity, an expression of the joy of living, rather than an attempt to do harm. To respond to infidelity with jealousy would, Hannah writes, be a "perversion of fidelity" and an attempt to "banish aliveness from the world." "True infidelity," she

writes, "is forgetting," which is "the only real sin, because it smothers the truth and all that is true."

Genuine fidelity, in other words, is not the same as sexual fidelity. To Hannah, fidelity was about continuity, about loyalty and reliability, about two people clinging on to each other and never letting go; it was about being faithful to what is true, genuine, and important. Hannah managed to reason her way to an understanding of fidelity that could accommodate Heinrich's infidelity.

WHY WAS THE IMPORTANCE of sexual fidelity and of monogamous marriage—even the nature of love itself—being questioned right then, in the 1920s and '30s? The answer is likely down to a few concurrent factors. Both the *carpe diem* attitude expressed in the Berliner approach to relationships and the wild years in Paris were a reaction to the spirit of the times. Europe had just survived a war and the economy was faltering—politics, too. People's lives were marked by uncertainty, by a sense that it could all be over tomorrow. This type of atmosphere gives rise to the impression that you should grab what you can while you still can. Live for today, because you might be dead tomorrow.

After the First World War, people began to challenge everything previously considered a fundamental societal institution: the flag, the throne, the altar. The nation, the royal family, and the church lost their power to enchant;

not one of these venerable institutions had been able to protect the populace from the horrors of war. In fact, they had been its cheerleaders. As people began to doubt these former heavyweights, other institutions, values, and ideals — such as marriage — were also called into question. Almost anything could be challenged or rejected, transmuted into a new form, freed from repression and moralism.

Another possible explanation for the era's interrogation of traditional values focuses on a liberation from religion and religious norms. The Russells, like de Beauvoir and Sartre, were staunch atheists. The Surrealists and the Bloomsbury Group also rejected religion. God did not exist, and with the death of God, the repressive morals governing sexuality, shame, and guilt also vanished. People were free to create their own norms and values, to write their own commandments, laws, and rules. Since Hannah and Heinrich were atheists too, God was not an authority in their lives; they were free to live how they liked.

And yet, reading Hannah's intellectual diary, it is clear that it pained her to see Heinrich direct his attention toward other women. Every relationship involves some kind of negotiation about space, freedom, and security. How much freedom can I give you without threatening my own? How free can I be without losing my sense of security? What if my beloved finds someone better than me? These risks are ever-present as a potential threat

when two people choose to open up their relationship to others.

Hannah expressed a strong need to belong with someone, to be part of the unit that she so beautifully describes in *The Human Condition*. She needed Heinrich. In a letter sent from Wiesbaden, dated February 8, 1950, she writes: "Snubby — for God's sake, you are my four walls." Heinrich replied swiftly from New York:

> You are right about the walls. I was the first (and this sets me apart from Jaspers) fully to experience and accept displacement, and could always say, "Where I am, I am not at home." But that is why I have established an eternal home here in this world, and not in a supernatural homeland of Zion, right in the middle of this world, with your help and that of friends, so that I too can say: "Where one or some of you are gathered, there is my homeland, and where you are with me, there is my home."

It takes faith to be able to cope with the knowledge that the person you love, the one who represents safety to you, is involved with someone else, laughing with someone else, being intimate with someone else. Faith that your love is strong enough, that your beloved's loyalty and belief that you are worth loving — that you have something no one else can give them — is strong enough. Faith that what the two of you have is so unique

that your beloved cannot find it with anyone else. Despite everything, this seems to have been what Hannah and Heinrich's relationship was like. Their intellectual fellowship, their friendship, their respect for one another, and the loyalty between them seems to have been of a very special ilk. Their shared history of escape and exile must also have bound them together.

Yet perhaps a balance of terror of some kind is also needed? An open relationship is likely easier to handle if both parties are involved in relationships on the side. Either way, it seems that Hannah's insecurity and fear of losing Heinrich to someone else vanished as she established a relationship of her own outside their marriage. In 1950, Hannah rekindled her relationship with Martin Heidegger, a decision that was supported by Heinrich. From that point on, Hannah and Martin would remain close until her death.

Twenty-Two

The Reunion

IN FORGIVENESS, THE TWO conflicting powers that dominated Hannah's life and thoughts—love and evil—came together. Without evil, without betrayal, insults, and lies, forgiveness would be unnecessary; without love, forgiveness would be impossible. Indeed, as she writes in *The Human Condition*, "only love has the power to forgive."

Forgiveness has a high moral value, and the person doing the forgiving can be described as loving and virtuous. A good person is expected to be magnanimous rather than bitter, hateful, or vengeful. Forgiveness is a central theme in the Judeo-Christian tradition, in which it is associated with the clearance of a debt. In the act of forgiveness, the sinner is transformed into a virtuous person, and the weight of guilt is lifted. Forgiveness, therefore, is a way to restore someone who has done wrong, and to heal a broken relationship.

When an insult has occurred, the balance between those involved is disturbed. A common belief is that the upset balance can only be restored through revenge or forgiveness, though in truth human existence is not quite so black and white. Revenge and forgiveness are the opposing reactions to an outrage, to evil, but a number of other attitudes and responses can exist in between. Someone who is unable or unwilling to forgive is not necessarily a bitter, hateful, vengeful person; the choice not to forgive can also be an expression of self-respect.

Forgiveness is a phenomenon that takes place between individuals who either are, or have been, in a relationship that has been damaged or broken somehow, whether by betrayal or offence. Hannah herself had mastered the difficult art of forgiveness, but her decision to forgive Martin Heidegger following his monumental betrayal is as difficult to understand as it is admirable. Where did she find the strength to absolve a man who had not only betrayed her on a personal level, but also actively supported an ideology that considered her and the people she belonged to as fundamentally less worthy than other human beings?

The answer, of course, is love—an utterly irrational emotion. Hannah's love for Martin was strong, overwhelming, and desperate. The power of the passion Hannah felt for Martin was stronger than the sorrow she felt at his betrayal; his rejection of her failed to dampen her feelings for him.

The last few letters they exchanged before Hannah fled Germany were bitter in tone. Hannah demanded answers about his attitude toward Hitler and the Nazi ideology; she wanted to know whether the rumours were true, whether he held anti-Semitic views. Martin's reply was indignant. He firmly denied treating his Jewish students any differently than the others, and he expressed concern that Hannah would listen to rumours of that kind. She, if anyone, must know that he had nothing against Jews.

As far as we know, Hannah never replied to that letter Martin sent her in early 1933, and in August that same year, she left Germany. All contact between her and Martin had been broken, but her fascination with him endured. She took his letters with her when she fled; somehow, their relationship was not yet over. Perhaps that is why she sought him out again, to reach closure, to demand answers, to force him to listen.

In 1949, four years after the war finally drew to a close, Hannah returned to Europe for the first time. She had been asked by the Jewish Cultural Reconstruction organization to track down and collect Jewish books, manuscripts, and other cultural artefacts, with the aim of documenting what was left of Jewish heritage in Europe. It proved to be an upsetting trip. Hannah arrived in Paris in November, and wrote to Heinrich that she had broken down in tears on seeing the city again: "God, this city is beautiful! You can't possibly fully remember."

She made her way to Bonn in December, and travelled around Germany—visiting Wiesbaden, Frankfurt, Würzburg, Nuremberg, Erlangen, and Heidelberg. In Basel, she met Karl Jaspers and his wife, and Martin Heidegger's name naturally came up. Karl, who had been deeply disappointed in Martin's behaviour during the 1930s, explained that he had rekindled contact with his former friend. Hannah told Karl about her relationship with Martin and was met by a relatively muted reaction; her friend was not particularly impressed by their love story.

On February 7, 1950, Hannah arrived in Freiburg. Despite her mixed feelings, she reached out to one of Martin's colleagues, Hugo Friedrich, a professor of Romance languages, to ask for his address. Hannah sent a message to Martin the very same day, telling him which hotel she was staying at, and suggesting that he come over to see her. At six thirty that evening, Martin himself showed up at Hannah's hotel with a written reply—the Heideggers still did not have a phone line at home—inviting her to come to his house at eight.

An earlier letter to Heinrich, dated January 3, had suggested that she was ambivalent about a possible meeting with her former lover: "I'll leave everything up to fate. His letters to Jaspers, the ones Jaspers showed me, just as they used to be: the same mix of genuineness and mendacity, or better still cowardice . . . with Jaspers I lost a little of my keenness for Heidegger."

We do not know exactly what happened between Martin and Hannah that evening—what they said to each other, what reproaches, explanations, and excuses were given—but it is clear from the letter Hannah sent to Martin on February 9, 1950, that she thought the meeting was a success:

> That evening and that [the next] morning are a confirmation of a whole life. In fact, a never-expected confirmation. When the waiter announced your name (I hadn't really expected you since I hadn't yet received your letter) it was as though suddenly time had stopped. Then, in a flash, I became aware—I have never before admitted it, not to myself and not to you and not to anyone else—that the force of my impulse, after Friedrich gave me your address, has mercifully saved me from committing the only truly unforgivable disloyalty, from mishandling my life. But you must know one thing (since we have not communicated much or very often) that had I done so, it would have been out of pride only—that is, out of pure, plain, crazy stupidity. Not for any reason.

There is no mistaking the intensity of Hannah's feelings here. It is as though she had reverted to being an infatuated eighteen-year-old. She expresses herself just as fatefully, just as romantically. And yet, twenty-six years had passed since their first meeting, and seventeen

since they last had any contact whatsoever. Hannah was now forty-three, with a blossoming academic career and a happy marriage. Martin was sixty, ejected from the circles in which he had once been the centre of attention, broken and weary following a protracted and exhausting denazification process. In the spring of 1946, he had suffered a breakdown, and was admitted to a rest home for a prolonged period.

Their situation, in other words, was completely different from the years during which Hannah was hopelessly in love with the celebrated and much older professor. By 1950, he was in the more vulnerable position. Hannah could have used her superior position to take revenge on him, to tell him what a pathetic, terrible person he was; Martin couldn't have known what she wanted from their meeting that evening—would she criticize him? Punish him? Tell him how much she hated him? Despite the obvious risk that the confrontation with his former lover would be deeply unpleasant, Martin chose to invite her to his home.

The letter Martin had written to Hannah the morning after her visit, on February 8, is warm and hopeful in tone:

> The unforeseen side of the beautiful evening yesterday and the brightening morning today remains. The essential always comes abruptly. In our language, "lightning" actually says: "look." But what is abrupt, in both good and evil, takes a long time to be resolved.

So I am sad that the hours were so short. And so I hope
even more gladly for your return, dear Hannah. It will
be the most beautiful thing of all, for now both the
early and the late have been brought purely into the
open. I know that you, too, are rejoicing in this purity,
and that you belong to us.

It is clear that Martin, too, was deeply affected by their
meeting. He, like Hannah, hoped her visit would be the
first of many. Their broken relationship had been healed;
everything had been "brought purely into the open," as
he put it. Elfriede, Martin's wife, was well aware of the
love he felt for Hannah, and she had also, according to
Martin, accepted the important position Hannah held in
his life. "In no way did my wife want to infringe on the
fate of our love," he wrote.

How did Hannah react to that, to the fact that the
woman she had so often expressed a dislike and distrust
for in letters and conversations with friends, suddenly
gave her blessing and accepted her husband's love for his
former student? With mixed feelings, in all likelihood.
On Martin's advice, she wrote a letter to Elfriede. The
tone is honest, and Hannah makes no attempt to mask
her feelings for the position Elfriede took during the war.
Nor does she apologize for having had an affair with her
husband. Despite all this, she ends the letter by professing
a desire to meet with Elfriede.

That February night in Freiburg became the first

chapter in part two of Hannah and Martin's story. Hannah seems to have rekindled some kind of flame in her former professor, because the very week after their reunion he sent her five poems dedicated to her. Martin then began to court her intensively, with frequent letters and poetry. His correspondence is romantic, verging on seductive; he compliments Hannah's appearance and reminds her of past moments, of books and music they had both enjoyed, of shared memories and past conversations.

On March 2, they met again. This time, Hannah stayed for four days. Judging by the letters they exchanged afterwards, Hannah spoke honestly, without sparing Martin, about the pain he had caused her, her sorrow at his betrayal, the loneliness she had felt while waiting for him, the anxiety she had experienced when he failed to get in touch, the fear of allowing love into her life after him. Martin returns to these conversations in several letters. In a letter from Messkirch dated May 4, for example, he writes:

> On March 2nd, as you came again, "the middle" occurred, bringing what had been into what endures. Time gathered into the fourth dimension of intimacy, as if we had stepped directly out of eternity — and returned to it. Whether this really is, you asked. Oh — even Being was crossed. But, closest one, you should know this: "*intending* and delicate" — nothing forgotten, with every contrary added to it whole — all

your pain, scarcely measured, and all my absence,
without denying it to myself, rang in a long ringing
of the bell of the world in our hearts. It rang in the
morning light, and for days afterward that moment
of the distant hearing of the now dawned anew for us.
You—Hannah—you.

She had forgiven him, and he was grateful for that.
Through her forgiveness, their painful history had evapor-
ated. Forgiveness, Hannah writes in *The Human Condition*,
"serves to undo the deeds of the past," and her forgive-
ness of Martin is a perfect example of this. It opened up
the possibility of a future. Through forgiveness, guilt is
lifted from the person who did wrong, and balance is
restored. Therein lies the power of forgiveness. If we were
unable to forgive one another, unburdening ourselves of
the consequences of our actions, our ability to act would
be limited to a single deed, and we would be prisoners
of its consequences for the rest of our lives. Forgiveness
releases that burden and liberates us from the past.

Forgiveness has a place in the interpersonal, private
relations between two people in either a friendship or a
romantic relationship. It is both an emotional and a moral
task. Forgiveness takes time, and it is painful. A damaged
relationship, a lost friend or lover, involves pain, and if the
broken relationship, the loss of the friend or lover, causes
more anguish than the betrayal that led to the problems,
then there is every reason to forgive.

Hannah and Martin maintained a warm relationship for the rest of their lives. They wrote to each other often, sometimes several times a month, sometimes a handful of times a year, and once the newly infatuated tone that dominated their correspondence that first year petered out, their discussions became more intellectual. Hannah asked her former supervisor for advice, they read each other's texts, and they traded both critiques and praise.

Hannah always tried to pay a visit to Martin and Elfriede whenever she was in Germany, and on several occasions Heinrich even joined her. Heinrich admired Martin as a philosopher, and he encouraged his wife to be part of his life. He understood what she meant to Martin, and he was impressed by the importance of his wife to the great philosopher. Heinrich knew, of course, about their history, but he thought of it as a youthful romance, an infatuation that belonged to the past. Martin Heidegger did not represent a threat to Heinrich and Hannah's marriage.

The two of them, Hannah and Heinrich, had created a life together. She could not live without Heinrich—he was her "four walls"—and the love she felt for him was built on a solid foundation of trust. There was loyalty between them, constancy, honesty, and friendship. Her attitude toward Martin was less easily defined—was it an obsession, an irrational dependency? Whatever the answer, her relationship with Heidegger could not have

continued without Heinrich's support. She was as wary
of Martin as she was sure of Heinrich, and were it not
for the fundamental sense of security that Heinrich gave
her, she never would have dared rekindle her relationship
with the other man.

But why was it so important for Hannah to have
Martin in her life? For several reasons, it seems. Martin
was, like Hannah, classically educated. He knew Greek
and Latin, had read the same thinkers as she had—he
had taught her, after all—and they had the same refer-
ence points. He matched her intellectually in a way no
one else could. They shared a past and memories of a
prewar Germany—a Europe—that had shaped their
thinking and development. It must also have been incred-
ibly flattering for Hannah to be the great philosopher's
chosen one, his soulmate. The fact he now needed her
must have spoken to her vanity.

Elfriede accepted Hannah in her life, though the two
women never became particularly good friends. They
were far too different, their competition for Martin
much too intense. Elfriede viewed the younger woman
with suspicion, but was smart enough to know that she
could not demand that Martin break off all contact with
Hannah again.

Elfriede also understood the important contribution
Hannah could play in restoring Martin's public image.
Following their reunion in 1950, Hannah took on the
role of Martin's unpaid agent. She made sure his books

were translated into English, negotiated contracts on his behalf, and spoke in his defence to those who were skeptical. To the Heideggers, her enthusiasm must have felt like a gift from above. Martin had been barred from teaching, and his previously bright prospects had been reduced to nothing as a result of his position during the war. Their finances were extremely volatile, and every book sold was an important boost to the family coffers.

Sure enough, Hannah proved crucial in the restoration of Martin's tarnished reputation. On one occasion, she even compared Martin to Thales, the ancient Greek philosopher who was so busy gazing at the stars that he did not notice he had fallen into a well. The essence of the comparison is obviously that Martin Heidegger was so preoccupied with philosophical thinking that he did not notice the worldly events to which he also happened to be contributing.

Hannah became his most enthusiastic defender, and she went to great lengths to excuse, smooth over, and downplay both Martin's association with Nazism and his explicit support for Hitler and the Third Reich. In her tribute to him, "Martin Heidegger at Eighty," she goes so far as to acquit him entirely. Hannah describes Martin's dealings with Nazism as "an error" that lasted just "ten short hectic months." She continues, writing that "Heidegger himself corrected his own 'error' more quickly and more radically than many of those who later sat in judgement over him," claiming that "he took

considerably greater risks than were usual in German literary and university life during that period."

Reading Hannah's unreserved tribute to Martin is heart-wrenching, not least because there is no empirical evidence for any of her claims, no documents or testimonies to back up her reassurances that Martin Heidegger never declared himself a supporter of Nazism. The loyalty and love she felt for Martin had blinded her. In 1969, when she wrote her tribute, it was common knowledge that he had been a member of NSDAP from May 1933 until the party ceased to exist in 1945. Hannah was also well aware of the infamous speech he gave in 1933, on being appointed rector in Freiburg, in which he patently endorsed some of the Nazi ideals, such as the restructuring of the universities along the new party line, and the significance of "blood and soil." This speech must have been on her mind when she chose to break off all contact with him, yet she relativized this by referring to his time as rector as "ten short hectic months." Hannah was obviously deeply influenced by Martin's version of his conduct before and during the war.

In the spring of 2014, many years after both Hannah's and Martin's deaths, the first three volumes of Martin's diaries were published, spanning the years between 1931 and 1941. These were followed late the next year by the diaries covering 1942–48. Martin himself referred to his diaries as "the black notebooks," a reference to their black waxed covers. The nickname took on another, more

fateful relevance upon publication, however, because Martin's own words demonstrate beyond all doubt that he was an enthusiastic member of the Nazi Party. He shared their fundamental principles and values, and he believed in the power and ability of Nazism to put Germany back on the right track. In his later diaries, it also becomes clear that Martin was aware of the Holocaust, and that he believed it was at least partly the Jews' own fault. If one reads Martin's black notebooks, it is very difficult not to conclude that he was a fully paid-up, devoted supporter of Adolf Hitler.

Hannah was not around to read the notebooks, of course, but how would she have processed the information contained within them if she had? We cannot know for sure, but it is not beyond the realm of possibility that she may have forgiven him. No one but Hannah can answer whether it was right or wrong of her to forgive Martin.

The American philosopher Margaret Holmgren argues that there are three questions that must always be asked whenever the idea of forgiveness is discussed: Is forgiveness compatible with self-respect? Is forgiveness compatible with respect for the person who did wrong as a moral agent? Is forgiveness compatible with respect for one's morals? She concludes that not only is forgiveness compatible with these three forms of respect, but respect also requires us to participate in the act of forgiving. If we really respect ourselves, we must do our utmost to develop the most respectable attitudes we are capable

of, and forgiveness is one such attitude. Respect for the person who did wrong as a moral being turns forgiveness into an appropriate response, since the wrongdoer's human dignity is both established and acknowledged in the act of forgiveness. Finally, Holmgren argues that respect for morals means that we must strive to develop a moral approach that also embraces those who have done wrong.

Holmgren makes some good points, but her reasoning can also be interrogated. Those who are quick to forgive may do so not, perhaps, out of self-respect, but rather as an expression of a *lack* of self-respect. Those who forgive easily may not think they have the right to make demands, and therefore subject themselves to the other's will rather than insisting on their own dignity and rights. In such a situation, forgiveness is more a burden than a virtue, because the person doing the forgiving fails to respect the moral value inherent in the self: that one is a goal in oneself.

Was Hannah's forgiveness too easily won? Did it signify a lack of self-respect? Forgiveness is an act of volition, and those who choose to forgive what in others' eyes seems unforgivable likely have good reasons for doing so. By choosing to forgive Martin, Hannah gave them both a second chance, and as far as we know, he gave her no reason to regret that decision. The pain of being without him for much of her life was greater than the pain he had already caused her.

Twenty-Three

Impossible Forgiveness

FORGIVENESS HAS TYPICALLY BEEN considered a religious or possibly psychological phenomenon, and therefore was often left to the theologians and behavioural scientists to argue over, but this changed after the Second World War and the Holocaust. How was the world—humankind— supposed to process such cruelty? Philosophers, political scientists, lawyers, and others began to take an interest in forgiveness as a possible response to evil, outrage, and injustice. Some saw it as a way to heal the world, while others argued that forgiveness of the perpetrators was not possible after the Holocaust.

Simon Wiesenthal survived multiple concentration camps, including Mauthausen, to which he was sent in 1945. During his imprisonment, he made a list of every Nazi he met during the war, drawing them from memory and keeping a note of their names and any other

information he could remember. Once the war ended, he founded the Jewish Historical Documentation Centre, an organization that aimed to document and track down Nazis in order to bring them to trial. Wiesenthal became known as "the Nazi hunter," and was responsible for bringing a large number of Nazi war criminals to justice—though he was always careful to point out that he was not looking for revenge.

But what about forgiveness?

In his autobiographical book *The Sunflower: On the Possibilities and Limits of Forgiveness*, Wiesenthal describes how he was summoned from the camp where he was being held, Lemberg, and taken by a nurse to visit a dying SS soldier. The man's last wish was to confess his sins to a Jew in the hope of being forgiven; he was deeply troubled by memories of the atrocities he had taken part in, and Simon had no choice but to listen to him talk about murdered women and children, burning Jews, and torture. Simon could not bring himself to decide whether he should forgive him or not, and ultimately chose silence, leaving the room without a word. Several years after the war, he still wasn't sure whether he had done the right thing. Perhaps he should have forgiven the dying soldier after all? Perhaps he had a moral duty to fulfill the man's last wish?

Simon Wiesenthal asked fifty-three people to respond to these questions, and presented their thoughts on the moral dilemma in *The Sunflower*. The men and women

who grappled with the issue were theologians, politicians, historians, psychologists, human rights activists, lawyers, Holocaust survivors, and convicted Nazi war criminals, and the vast majority argued that Wiesenthal did the right thing by not forgiving the man. Interestingly, Albert Speer—Minister of Armaments in Nazi Germany, who was convicted of crimes against humanity—was among those who took this view. He argued that the crimes committed by the Nazis were much too great to be forgiven. Others, like Jean Améry, himself a survivor, were less sure, perhaps because of the uncertainty around the concept of forgiveness: what exactly does it mean in this context? A handful of respondents, including the Dalai Lama and Desmond Tutu, argued that the loving thing would have been to forgive.

How would Hannah have responded to Simon Wiesenthal's question? She describes forgiveness as a "remedy for irreversibility" in *The Human Condition* and writes that forgiveness has the power to "undo the deeds of the past." Forgiveness has the power to liberate both victims and perpetrators from past events. But would she have chosen to free the dying SS soldier from his anguish? That seems doubtful. Hannah was a believer in the idea that there are certain acts—and individuals— that are unforgivable. In *Responsibility and Judgment*, for example, she writes about forgiveness in relation to *skandalon*—that is, genuinely evil deeds. She argues that we can choose between vengeance and punishment or

forgiveness, but there are certain acts so terrible that it is impossible to come to a reasonable, just punishment. The harm caused by these acts cannot be measured, and therefore falls outside the framework of not only punishment, but also forgiveness.

After all, as Hannah writes, when we forgive, it is a person being forgiven. A person who has carried out genuinely evil deeds and caused immeasurable cruelty cannot be forgiven because they, through their actions, have robbed themselves of their personhood: "In rootless evil there is no person left whom one could forgive." Hannah's argument takes its basis from Kant's reasoning around evildoers who bring punishment on themselves through their actions, erasing their own inherent human dignity by violating the categorical imperative. They invalidate their own humanity, meaning there is no longer anyone to forgive.

Acts that fall under the banner of *skandalon* are beyond the power of humankind to remedy. Hannah writes that those who have carried out such genuinely evil deeds cannot change or be rehabilitated through either punishment or forgiveness. Their deeds, their acts of evil, are a crime against the world order itself. It would be better for them "that a millstone were hanged about [their] neck, and [they] cast into the sea," Hannah writes, quoting the Gospel of Luke.

The evil described here is obviously of a different nature than the evil that manifests in betrayal, lies, infidelity, and

broken promises. Perhaps we should reserve the concept of "evil" for only the most serious affronts to human dignity? The evil that took shape in the Holocaust—a well-organized, considered, methodical genocide—is something entirely different from the betrayal Heidegger exposed Hannah to. Yes, he sympathized with Nazi ideology, but he had no blood on his hands.

If forgiveness is impossible, then what is possible? Does someone who refuses to forgive become a prisoner of the past, preoccupied by thoughts of revenge? It is not possible to forgive a genocide like the Holocaust, but it is possible to reconcile oneself with what happened. While forgiveness involves the blame being lifted from the culprit's shoulders, reconciliation suggests that the person experiencing reconciliation maintains that what happened was wrong, yet accepts that it happened. The Swedish social psychologist Lasse Dencik describes the difference as follows:

> Reconciliation is not the same as forgiveness. The fact that the majority of my family was murdered in the Nazi concentration camps is something I must reconcile myself with, but I will never be willing nor able to forgive the Nazis who murdered them.

Twenty-Four

Love Without Pain

HOW DOES A PERSON endure a life that contains as much pain as Hannah's did? One answer must come down to Hannah herself, to the type of woman she was. Hannah was someone who took things very seriously, but she also possessed the ability to see the absurdity in any given situation. She laughed frequently, and had, as intelligent people often do, a good sense of humour. Hannah was also able to appreciate the small, everyday treasures of life. Giving in was not in her nature. She struggled, protested, and worked hard because she believed that it was her duty, and because the alternative — staying quiet and admitting defeat — was impossible.

Another answer focuses on the people she surrounded herself with, on Heinrich and her mother — two people who were unfailingly loyal to Hannah over

the years—and on the many dear friends she had. Her friends cared for her as she cared for them.

Friendship is a particular form of love, free from the anxieties inherent in passionate, romantic love. Hannah touches upon this special type of love in her doctoral thesis, *Der Liebesbegriff bei Augustin* (*Love and Saint Augustine*). Saint Augustine uses just one term to describe love, *appetitus*, but Hannah claims to have found other discussions of the nature of love in his writing, descriptions of love that are reciprocal rather than demanding: neighbourly love. This reciprocal love differs from the desire typical of erotic or romantic love. It also differs from the more altruistic, generous, self-effacing love. Neighbourly love is characterized instead by reciprocity and co-operation—a friendly love.

What type of relationship is friendship, exactly? Like love, it requires nourishment and attention, but it lacks the pain and suffering that comes with romantic or erotic love. Friendship is love without pain, but that does not mean that it is a relationship free from demands. Epicurus writes that friendship must be cultivated as though it were a garden. And it can also, as Hannah herself experienced, be dramatic and lead to disappointment.

According to Hans Jonas, Hannah had a rare "genius for friendship." To paraphrase Epicurus, she knew how to tend to friendships. Hannah was highly reliable, a loyal and considerate companion—as illustrated by the many letters she wrote to her friends across the world, not least

those she sent to American author Mary McCarthy. The letters Hannah and Mary exchanged over several decades have since been published in *Between Friends: The Correspondence of Hannah Arendt and Mary McCarthy, 1949–1975*.

Hannah and Mary first met in 1944, at the Murray Hill Bar in Manhattan, and clicked immediately. Barely three years after arriving in the United States, Hannah had begun to establish herself as a writer, and was on her way to becoming part of the large circle of New York intellectuals in which Mary McCarthy was already a key member. Mary, who was six years younger than Hannah, had been orphaned as a young girl, when her parents died during the 1918 flu epidemic. She grew up under poor conditions with her father's Catholic parents, and was subjected to abuse by an uncle. Mary had a thirst for knowledge, and she managed to escape her impoverished background by studying. She attended Vassar College and began to write for various intellectual journals, going on to make a name for herself as a liberal critic of both communism and McCarthyism. By the time she and Hannah met, she had already published her first—critically acclaimed—novel, *The Company She Keeps*.

Mary appreciated Hannah's skeptical nature and European education, and Hannah found joy in Mary's American temperament, which she thought less gloomy and more easygoing than those of so many in the old world. "Their discussions are without fanaticism and

their arguments are accessible to a large number of people," Hannah wrote about her new American friends in a letter to Karl Jaspers in 1946. "Each intellectual here is sure as a matter of principle that he is, as an intellectual, in opposition...he does not worship the God of Success." In her disappointment as she was leaving Germany, Hannah had made a promise to herself never to spend time with academics again, having developed a deep sense of contempt for elitist and opportunistic intellectuals — yet she regained hope for freedom of thought in the United States.

Both Hannah and Mary were temperamental, and they shared the same sharp sense of humour — though this could have brought an end to their burgeoning friendship at a very early stage. At a dinner party in 1945, Mary made a tasteless remark about Hitler that left Hannah furious. Mary had said that she felt sorry for Hitler, who was so absurd that he wanted to be liked by his victims. "How can you say such a thing in front of me, one of Hitler's victims," Hannah shot back, "a person who has been in a concentration camp?" She then turned on her heel and left.

It took Hannah three years to forgive Mary for that thoughtless remark. "Let's end this nonsense now. We think so much alike," she eventually told Mary when they ended up on the same side of the debate at a seminar. Mary immediately and unreservedly apologized, and Hannah confessed that she had never actually been in a

concentration camp, but in an internment camp. After that incident, the two women were loyal to each other for the rest of their lives. They didn't have to put on an act when they were together, pretending to be someone or something else.

In January 1965, Mary wrote to Hannah from Paris:

> Dear Hannah, when *will* we see each other? I miss you so much. In Paris, I have no real friends; that is simply the fact. My friends like Sonia [Orwell] and Anjo Lévi have to be handled with so much tact or rather with so much suppressed impatience that you are never at ease with them.

A person does not need to put on airs with a genuine friend; there is no need to weigh your words or worry about putting your foot in it. A real friend has a fundamental faith and belief in you; you can relax and feel comfortable around them, thinking aloud, sharing unfinished thoughts, and expressing all kinds of hopes, fears, and ideas.

One of the many topics the two friends discussed in their letters was friendship itself, exploring the importance of conversation in relationships. It is only when you share details of your life with another person, with a friend, that you in some sense come to understand your past and present. Our stories need someone to listen to them, a kind ear to receive them. As Austrian-Israeli

philosopher Martin Buber writes, we only become *I* in the meeting with *thou*.

"Life is not what one lived, but what one remembers and how one remembers it in order to recount it," writes Gabriel García Márquez in *Living to Tell the Tale*. By telling others about ourselves and our experiences, our lives, we are also telling ourselves the story. As Hannah wrote to Mary in 1971: "One can't say how life is ... except by telling the tale."

The philosopher of religion Don Cupitt argues that human life consists of multiple short stories. We tell our lives, evoking meaning and identity, giving ourselves both a past and a future. We come into being through our memories and what we choose to remember, how we share them — and with whom.

Aristotle, one of the philosophers Hannah frequently turned to throughout her life, discussed the nature and value of friendship in several works. Humans cannot, he argued, be either rational or good on their own; they need other people, friends, in order to be human. The man who can live alone, Aristotle writes in *The Politics*, is "either an animal or a god." Humans are by nature social creatures who are active within society and seek out friends, and their practical wisdom, or *phronesis* — good judgement and the ability to make reasoned decisions — can, according to Aristotle, only be developed through friendship.

In *Nicomachean Ethics*, Aristotle describes friendship

as the desire to do good deeds for another person—to wish another well. Aristotle also argued that friendship is necessary for our moral development. We see ourselves reflected in the other, and a good friend can make us into a somewhat better person. Having good friends has always been considered a fortune, even a necessity.

Aristotle writes that by having friends, human beings have greater resources both intellectually and practically. Hannah understood and experienced this on countless occasions during her life, not least during her years in exile in France, when she relied on her friends' help as they relied on hers. Friendship, or the ability to exercise friendliness, is in Aristotle's eyes a virtue, a character trait that helps us to live good lives. Friendship, he writes, is not just necessary, it is also noble. With the help of our friends, we become better people—at least if we choose them with care.

Aristotle's arguments about friendship focus on male friendship, of course. In his intellectual world, women broadly did not exist, and his ideal is therefore a male, courtly type of friendship. Between such equal men, three types of friendship are possible: those based on utility, those based on pleasure or delight, and those grounded in virtue. But is there any difference between male and female friendship? I suspect not. Some people use relationships to gain advantages for themselves, and therefore choose friends they can benefit from. Others focus on pleasure. According to Aristotle, neither the

utility- nor desire-based friendships are long-lasting. The deepest and most enriching friendships can be found between two people who have chosen each other because they appreciate the other's merits. They can grow together, becoming better, wiser people than would have been possible on their own. Maybe, just maybe, this is the key distinction between love and friendship: love is fickle, whereas friendship is reliable.

The nature of friendship was a subject that also fascinated Heinrich. Taking Aristotle's writing as his starting point, he discussed love and friendship in a number of lectures. In Heinrich's eyes, friendship was like love without *eros* (desire). In the very last lecture he ever gave, in 1968, he spoke about friendship, suggesting that it emerges when *eros* is no longer in the way. The erotic desire that occurred when the two people first met is no longer a driving force — what matters in a friendship is that two personalities respect each other, give each other space, accept each other as they are, and aid the other's development.

Hannah and Heinrich's family was made up of friends, of people they had known in Germany and others they had met during their exile in France or upon arrival in the United States. Hannah in particular considered her friends central to her life. She dedicated her books to them, contributed to tribute and party speeches, wrote profiles of them, and helped to disseminate their works, quotes, and stories. She kept up contact, remembered

their birthdays, sent condolences when they were griev-
ing, wrote letters and mailed parcels, cooked and invited
them to dinner, listened, and gave good advice — but
never took pity on them. She was, as Elisabeth Young-
Bruehl writes in her biography of Hannah, *Hannah Arendt:
For Love of the World*, "fluent in the language of friendship."

AFTER THEY MOVED to the United States, Hannah and
Heinrich surrounded themselves with writers, poets,
artists, and other intellectuals. Some were new acquaint-
ances, and others, like Peter Huber, were old friends who
had also been forced to flee Europe.

Hannah and Heinrich's friends often gathered at their
home on Riverside Drive to eat, drink, and talk. At the
heart of the apartment was a large living room, furnished
with sofas and armchairs, and several small tables laden
with ashtrays, cigarettes, matches, and bowls of nuts and
candy. The walls were lined with overburdened book-
shelves, and Hannah's desk was positioned in front of the
large window that looked out onto the Hudson River.
It was a home created for socializing and work. In the
summer, the group of friends would leave New York
together to continue their conversations elsewhere — by
the sea, or in the mountains.

Despite the fact that Hannah surrounded herself with
many close friends, she also sought out the dead by read-
ing their books, trying to understand their arguments,

and allowing them to influence her thinking. In her anthology *Men in Dark Times*, Hannah wrote profiles of ten of her friends, people who meant a lot to her and her intellectual development. Several of those featured are people she was still in contact with at the time — Karl Jaspers, for example — but others, like Walter Benjamin, were sorely missed friends who had been snatched away from her and the world. Some are friends she had met through literature but never in reality, like Rosa Luxemburg, who died in 1919.

One of the people who seems to have had the greatest impact on Hannah is Rahel Varnhagen, who died long before Hannah was even born, in 1833. Born in Berlin in 1771, Rahel was, like Hannah, Jewish. She was highly educated and extremely gifted, and she hosted a legendary salon in which the intellectual and academic elite of the day gathered. Hegel, Schlegel, Fichte, Schleiermacher, and the Humboldt brothers are just a few of the illustrious figures who surrounded her.

Hannah used Rahel Varnhagen's letters to write an ambitious biography of her, and thus spent many years interacting with a woman who had died a century earlier. Rahel proved a loyal friend during the lonely, anxious years before Hannah left Germany, a period during which she spent far too much time waiting for letters or visits from Martin. This was also the period in which Hannah seriously began to think about what her Jewish heritage meant to her.

Here, too, Rahel was there to hold her hand. Like Hannah a hundred years later, she had struggled with her Jewish identity. Hannah begins her book on Rahel by quoting what are alleged to be her final words: "The thing which all my life seemed to me the greatest shame, which was the misery and misfortune of my life—having been born a Jewess—this I should on no account now wish to have missed."

LITERARY CRITIC WAYNE BOOTH describes reading as a relationship, and he argues that we should view this relationship as a kind of friendship. Booth is particularly interested in literature's effect on the reader—in what happens in the meeting between reader and text—and in a reference to Aristotle's classification of the various types of friendship, he argues that we should also choose our literary friends with care. The books we read and the people we meet in them contribute to the shaping of our worldview and our values, deepening our understanding of both ourselves and others.

Booth has a point in saying that what we read has an influence on us, yet we must also go beyond reading those we like and admire by reading the darker, less pleasant pages in life, trying to understand the people whose choices and actions we feel dislike—even disgust—for. Hannah wrote about Adolf Eichmann not because she thought he was a model citizen, but because she wanted

to understand him and his motives. In this context, we should point out that understanding is not the same as excusing, and even less a synonym for forgiving.

Hannah's book on Eichmann and her theory about the banality of evil left her isolated. Though not all of her friends actively chose to distance themselves from her, she sensed that many were avoiding her. While she was a celebrated, highly praised intellectual, they had been happy to be seen with Hannah and basked in her glory. As her popularity waned, however, they were no longer so keen—once they no longer stood to gain by being her friend, they simply disappeared. The friends that remained were those who had chosen Hannah out of respect for her merits, not because of how they bene- fited by bragging about being the great Hannah Arendt's friend.

Heinrich was still there by her side, of course. Mary McCarthy, too. Her loyalty didn't waver for even a second, and she defended Hannah against all the criti- cism levelled at her. Mary was the very type of person everyone wants and needs in their life: faithful, honest, and loyal. She also had the ability—and was brave enough—not simply to say what Hannah wanted to hear, but what she needed to. As the Eichmann controversy unfolded, Mary was there, loyal to Hannah but also ready to provide firm advice. She felt that Hannah needed to explain herself and straighten out the misunderstandings and misinterpretations that were becoming increasingly

grotesque — something Hannah long refused to do, convinced that the whole thing would soon blow over. But it didn't, not for many years.

While Hannah was deeply frustrated at being so misunderstood, Mary was one of the few people she could confide in: "I can no longer trust myself to keep my head and not to explode. What a risky business to tell the truth on a factual level without theoretical and scholarly embroidery," she wrote to Mary in despair in September 1963, months into the controversy. Mary replied with an attempt at an explanation. It is clear that Mary's thoughts were dominated by the hostile attacks Hannah had been subjected to, and that she was trying to understand what it was all about. In October 1963, Mary wrote:

> It occurs to me that a desire to make a sensation has taken precedence in New York over everything else. The literary and intellectual world is turning into a series of Happenings, like the one at the Edinburgh Theatre Conference where a naked girl was introduced into the auditorium. The editors have become show-men and the reader is a spectator in a circus ring.

Karl Jaspers also stood firm by Hannah's side during the worst of the storm, despite being on the other side of the Atlantic. Hannah thought of him as something of a father figure, a link to the past, someone who represented

continuity and stability in her life. Karl was one of Hannah's most long-standing friends; he had known her since she was an unknown, inquiring young student, and Hannah was overjoyed when they re-established contact after the war. In a letter to Kurt Blumenfeld, she wrote the following about their rekindled friendship: "Trust is not an empty delusion, and in the long run it is the only thing that can assure one that one's private world is not also a Hell." Unfortunately, Kurt Blumenfeld would disappoint Hannah, but Karl Jaspers did not. He lived up to the faith and trust Hannah put in him.

Karl Jaspers read Hannah's articles about Eichmann, and he even wrote an introductory text for her book when it was published in Germany. His support and encouragement meant a lot to Hannah, and the Eichmann controversy failed to damage their friendship. If anything, it made it stronger. When Hannah apologized for something Heinrich had said by claiming that he struggled to keep his temper in check when she was attacked, Jaspers replied:

> I can understand Heinrich's anger. You have hit many people's most sensitive nerve endings — a lie in their very existence — and they hate you . . . The truth will be beaten to death, as Kierkegaard said of Socrates and Jesus. Now, it has not come to this and it will not. But you have been given a *fama* [bad reputation], which, for you, is not the right thing, detestable. In

the long run your character will, of course, prevail
and triumph radiantly.

You could say that Jaspers was proved right.

Twenty-Five

Amor Mundi:
Love of the World

DEATH IS THE SHARED FATE of humankind. We are all going to die, to be wrenched away from everything we cling to, love, and desire. Each of us will be robbed of the future.

In her thesis on the concept of love in the writings of Saint Augustine, the first aspect of love that Hannah analyzes is desire, a dimension of love that is geared toward the future, because it expresses a longed-for direction. We desire that which is good for us, but as soon as we possess the thing we once craved, we are struck down by the fear of losing it. Once we have achieved the thing we long for, once we possess what we desire, we are immediately overtaken by the feeling that it could all be lost. Desire-love provides no guarantees, no security. It is inextricably linked to the fear of loss, something Hannah

experienced in her relationship with Martin. She wrote: "The trouble with human happiness is that it is constantly beset by fear. It is not the lack of possessing but the safety of possession that is at stake."

This remark is, above all, applicable to life itself. Since the premise of earthly life is that it is finite—death catches up with us all—Hannah argues that we live in constant fear of losing our lives. Life is, in a fundamental sense, characterized by fear.

Life is a subject we know much about, but we know very little about death. It is, as the philosopher Vladimir Jankélévitch wrote, unthinkable: I cannot imagine a world without me, and I cannot imagine not existing. Thoughts of death are something of a contradiction: "Neither my birth nor my death can appear to me as experiences of my own," wrote another philosopher, Maurice Merleau-Ponty. Sigmund Freud, the famous psychoanalyst, seems to have shared this view: "We cannot, indeed, imagine our own death; whenever we try to do so we find that we survive ourselves as spectators." And Edgar Morin, the philosopher-sociologist whose study of ideas about death is considered groundbreaking, argues that all notions about death are utterly empty, because they are built on the unthinkable, the unknowable.

Jankélévitch claims that death is humankind's greatest and most fundamental fear. Everything we do, we do to avoid death, and the closer to it we come, the more we fight it. Almost as an echo of this idea, cultural

anthropologist Ernest Becker describes the fear of death as the source of all human fear and all human actions, in his prizewinning book *The Denial of Death*. People are constantly trying to deny death, to overcome it—by having children, by finding a new lover, or by buying a new motorcycle; by jogging, losing weight, or becoming a vegetarian. Anything to keep their fear of death in check.

And yet we are all, inevitably, going to die. As humans, we are acutely aware of the fact that we must die, but we are incapable of understanding our own deaths. Perhaps what Freud wrote is true, and each of us is subconsciously convinced of our own immortality. Still, the essential, unthinkable realization that our lives are not eternal is a fundamental experience. The misery of mortality, paradoxically, makes us godlike. The knowledge that we will one day pass away leads to creation—we preserve the past, our memories, and create a future to put off death. Life is valuable precisely because it ends. That insight, sociologists such as Zygmunt Bauman have argued, is the root of all human creativity. We would not have written novels, constructed buildings, or come up with religious ideals if we were ignorant of our own mortality.

The insight into the finite nature of our existence, and the terror it strikes in us, is the basis of religion. After all, religion offers us the one thing we desire most: the promise of eternal life; a reassurance that it does not end after all, that there is some kind of continuation. Religion gives

us hope. Hannah discusses both desire and hope in *Love and Saint Augustine*, arguing that it is a misconception that hope can allay our fear of death: "What ultimately stills the fear of death is not hope or desire, but remembrance and gratitude." Remembrance and gratitude: these are the cure for a fear of death.

Life is what takes place between birth and death. Life, which is finite and therefore endlessly valuable. My life and your life and the life we create; living is what we do together. It is only by living alongside others that we become people. We share the world, and we are all subject to mortality. In that sense, death is democratic — no one can escape it; it is equally merciless with each of us. Death, therefore, is more just than life, because life — the time between birth and death — is anything but just. We live in wildly different realities, under hugely different conditions.

How then, should we live? What does it mean to be human? What is a good life; what are good, just actions? How should we treat one another? How should we live in an imperfect world? *"Amor mundi* — why is it so hard to love the world?"* Hannah asks in her intellectual diary. What does it mean to love the world? Is it even possible? In *The Human Condition*, she writes: "Love, by its very nature, is unworldly, and it is for this reason rather than its rarity that it is not only apolitical but antipolitical, perhaps the most powerful of all antipolitical human forces."

When Hannah talks about loving the world, she means something other than the love existing between humans. To love the world is more about understanding and reconciling oneself with it. *Amor mundi* is an attitude, a direction of travel that focuses on forgiveness, acceptance, and reconciliation. In order to live in a world where the Holocaust was possible, we must understand and accept what happened, just as we must understand what is happening today.

Loving the world means taking care of life so that it can continue to exist. As we reflect, we must therefore, Hannah argues, pay attention to what has happened, to what is happening, and what may happen in the future. We must never forget, but neither must we lose ourselves to nostalgia. We must be able to love the world as it is, in all its imperfection; we must live with our memories and remember what we have to be thankful for.

Twenty-Six

Reconciliation

ON MARCH 19, 1962, Hannah had a premonition of her own death. The taxi driving her home through Central Park was hit by a truck, and she was taken to Roosevelt Hospital in an ambulance, bloodied but conscious. She was calm when Heinrich arrived at the hospital, but she had also sustained injuries that would trouble her for several months: a concussion, fractured ribs, bleeding in both eyes, a cracked tooth, swelling, cuts, and bruises. The shock of the accident had also damaged her heart.

In a letter to Mary McCarthy describing the event, Hannah wrote:

> I awoke in the car and became conscious of what had happened. I tried out my limbs, saw that I was not paralyzed and could see with both eyes; then tried out my memory — very carefully, decade by decade,

poetry, Greek and German and English, then tele-
phone numbers. Everything all right. The point was
that for a fleeting moment I had the feeling that it
was up to me whether I wanted to live or to die. And
though I did not think that death was terrible, I also
thought that life was quite beautiful and that I['d]
rather take it.

She described the same feelings in a letter to Karl Jaspers:
"It seemed to me that for a moment I had my life in my
hands. I was quite calm: death seemed to me natural,
in no way a tragedy or, somehow, out of the order of
things. But, at the same time, I said to myself: if it is
possible to do so decently, I would really like, still, to
stay in this world."

Hannah had reconciled herself with the world. Ten
years earlier, in a letter to Kurt Blumenfeld, she wrote
that "if only world history were not so awful, it would
be a joy to live," but by 1962 she had decided that she
would "really like, still, to stay in this world" and that
life was "quite beautiful." She was not afraid of death,
but she wanted to live for a while yet. And live she did.
Hannah lived another thirteen years after the car acci-
dent — thirteen productive, harmonious years that were,
sadly, darkened by Heinrich's faltering health. He fell ill
in September 1963, and Hannah struggled with the real-
ization that he would likely die before she did: "We have
been together for twenty-eight years and life without him

would be unthinkable," she wrote to Mary around the time he fell ill.

Heinrich recovered on that particular occasion, and they enjoyed another seven years together before he died on October 30, 1970. The couple had friends over to dinner the evening before, and Heinrich had been his usual vociferous self. He joined in the discussions, ate, and enjoyed his usual serving of schnapps. During lunch the next day, he felt a sudden, continuous pain in his chest. A panicked Hannah called for an ambulance, but Heinrich was calm. He simply held Hannah's hand and said, "This is it."

He died that evening, at Mount Sinai Hospital, with Hannah and his friend Peter Huber by his side. Peter, who had known Heinrich since his Berlin years and had been interned with him in Villemalard, documented his last few hours with his camera. The next evening, Hannah and Heinrich's friends gathered in their apartment. "How am I to live now?" Hannah asked, disoriented and virtually paralyzed by grief. Her loneliness and longing were almost physically tangible.

Heinrich's funeral took place at the Riverside Chapel on November 4. Several of his colleagues from Bard College gave eulogies, as did two of his students and a number of friends. One of those who spoke quoted Plato's *Apology of Socrates*: "But now it is time to go away, I to die and you to live. Which of us goes to a better thing is unclear to everyone except to the god."

Hannah often returned to those words after Heinrich's death. She makes reference to them in a letter sent to Martin three weeks after Heinrich's funeral:

> Between two people, sometimes, how rarely, a world grows. It is then one's homeland; in any case, it was the only homeland we were willing to recognize. This tiny microworld where you can always escape from the world, and which disintegrates when the other has gone away. I go now and am quite calm and think: *away*.

With Heinrich's death, the universe he and Hannah had created, the context that had brought Hannah a sense of security since they first met in Paris in the 1930s, also died. Hannah and Heinrich had shared joy and sorrow, they had moved to a new continent together, mastering an unfamiliar culture and language. They had lived in happy symbiosis. Their good friend Randall Jarrell, a writer from Nashville, once described them as the "dual monarchy," a kingdom with two rulers. Two stubborn, strong-willed monarchs who managed to reign together for thirty-five years. They had, as Hannah wrote, created a world of their own, a country that was theirs. But she was now alone, and the country that had previously represented security, her shield against the rest of the world, had vanished. Where could she turn with her sorrow?

In the weeks following Heinrich's death, Hannah's friends made sure she was not left alone in their spacious apartment on Riverside Drive. Anne Mendelsohn Weil flew in from France to be with Hannah that winter, working alongside Hannah's maid, Sally Davis, to keep the home in order, to do the shopping, and to make sure Hannah ate dinner every day. Anne also made sure Hannah kept to her usual social routines. With Anne's help, Hannah invited her friends over to celebrate the new year, as she did every year, and she also invited her students to dinner once they reached the end of their course on Kant.

Despite everything, life went on. Hannah took each day as it came. In a letter to Mary, she wrote:

> I am not tired, or not much tired, just exhausted. I function all right, but know that the slightest mishap could throw me off balance. I don't think I told you that for ten long years I had been constantly afraid that just such a sudden death would happen. This fear frequently bordered on real panic. Where the fear was and the panic there is now sheer emptiness.

Hannah managed the loss of the man who personified the concept of "life partner" in much the same way she managed all other sorrows and crises: by analyzing and systematizing both her reactions and her new circumstances. She kept up her routines and kept moving

forward, even if it was on slightly unsteady legs. Hannah continued to lecture, write, and fulfill her duties, but she did it all with diminished enthusiasm. She had less of a thirst for social interaction than before, and sought out peace and quiet increasingly often, preferring to withdraw from others in order to think and write.

Hannah's life was full of departures. She had been uprooted and had started afresh several times, leaving behind countries and languages, having to reconstruct her life time and time again. After Heinrich's death, she had no desire to start over. She did not want to build anything new. She wanted to rest in what had been. Shortly after Heinrich died, she was visited by the poet W. H. Auden, who, to Hannah's dismay, proposed. Hannah was both surprised and embarrassed by his proposal—Auden thought they may as well get hitched because they were both on their own—and gently but firmly declined the offer. She had no desire for a new marriage.

Life is often depicted as a journey from beginning to end, with grief, old age, and illness each a trip into the unknown. After Heinrich's death, Hannah found herself in a completely new existence—a "lonely freedom," as Elisabeth Young-Bruehl puts it. Yet again, Hannah was in exile, only this time it was existential. Those who find themselves in exile have not chosen to leave their comfortable, comprehensible lives, their homelands; they are, in a sense, homeless, in an alien environment,

surrounded by a language they do not speak, people they do not know, and traditions, scents, and tastes they have never experienced before. Those in exile are in a reality they cannot easily process, and they do not know when — or if — they will ever be able to return to the life that is theirs. The place where they are themselves. Where they can be as they were.

The last few years of Hannah's life were tinged, as they are for the lives of the majority of us, with loss and death. In December 1973, following the deaths of two close friends, she wrote to Mary:

> I must admit that I mind this relentless defoliation (or deforestation) process. As though to grow old does not mean, as Goethe said, "gradual withdrawal from appearance" — which I do not mind — but the gradual (or rather sudden) transformation of a world with familiar faces (no matter, foe or friend) into a kind of desert, populated by strange faces. In other words, it is not me who withdraws but the world that dissolves — an altogether different proposition.

Like Hannah, Jean Améry describes aging in terms of alienation. As we age, we no longer recognize ourselves or the world around us; we become strangers not only to the world in which we live, but also to our bodies and faces. We are, he writes in *On Aging*, homeless in both time and space, and no longer know who or what we are.

Simone de Beauvoir expresses the same sense of alienation and disorientation in *Force of Circumstance*: "When I read in print Simone de Beauvoir, it is a young woman they are telling me about, and who happens to be me." Studying herself in the mirror, she no longer sees Simone de Beauvoir looking back at her, but an older, unfamiliar woman whose face she no longer recognizes. "I loathe my appearance now: the eyebrows slipping down towards the eyes, the bags underneath, the excessive fullness of the cheeks, and that air of sadness round the mouth that wrinkles always bring... when I look, I see my face as it was, attacked by the pox of time for which there is no cure."

Aging is a prelude to unavoidable death, and it involves the gradual decline of the body. Our vision, hearing, and agility all worsen, and such a degeneration can be painful to bear. For Simone de Beauvoir, the loss of her once attractive features was difficult; the transformation from a beautiful woman to an old one hard to take. For a woman who is used to others' glances, to attracting attention and interest, aging makes her feel invisible. People no longer look at her with desire.

Hannah was an attractive woman, the kind of woman who commanded a room the moment she stepped into it, and yet she does not seem to have grieved for the loss of her beauty. Still, it is clear that she did not appreciate the limitations that aging and the illnesses that came with it brought to her life. As a consequence of the car

accident she was involved in during the 1960s, Hannah
suffered heart problems that worsened the older she got.
In December 1971, she wrote to Mary following a visit
to the doctor's office: "the usual talk—slow down, stop
smoking, etc. Since I certainly am not going to live for
my health, I'll do what I think is right."

Doing what she thought was right meant continuing
as before. Hannah did not cancel any engagements, and
she refused to stop smoking. Ever since she was a young
woman, she had always had a cigarette between her lips
when she wrote, and it was a practice she continued
throughout her life. Hannah could not write without
smoking—or that was what she believed, anyway.

Hannah spent the last few years of her life working
on the manuscript for *The Life of the Mind*, which would
be published after her death. The book is, in essence, an
examination of good government. Mirroring Plato in
the *Republic*, Hannah uses human abilities as an analogy
for how the various parts of a good state work in union.
The three abilities Hannah takes as her starting point are
thinking, willing, and judging. Discussing judgement
in relation to thinking and will, she makes reference to
Cicero's *De Senectute* (*On Old Age*). She cites Cicero, who
has Cato the Elder say that it "is not by muscle, speed,
or physical dexterity that great things are achieved, but
by reflection, force of character, and judgement; in these
qualities old age is usually not only not poorer, but is
even richer."

Hannah had read Simone de Beauvoir's book on aging, *The Coming of Age*, and did not share de Beauvoir's dystopian view of aging. Nor did she share society's fixation on youth. Hannah wanted to emphasize the qualities inherent in aging, the abilities that only a person who has lived a long life possesses. She wrote that aging involves a loss of future, but that this need not necessarily provoke anxiety. Instead, the lack of a future can give rise to reflection and reconciliation — time to balance the books and understand one's life backwards, as Kierkegaard put it. Aging makes it possible to contemplate the meaning of the past, and to tell your story to yourself.

From the perspective of the mind, aging is a time for introspection and meditation; a time when the exacting needs of self-interest fade away and we are freed from all ideological inhibitions. We are, as Hannah put it in a letter to Mary, "free like a leaf in the wind" — free from all loyalty and demands.

THE MIDDLE AGES SAW the proliferation of various *ars moriendi*, texts that focused on the art of dying. Death was a journey that was given utmost importance, and dying took time. A good death, therefore, was a drawn-out, painful one: a period in which the dying could be remembered and reconciled, with both themselves and others, with their lives. Hannah's final years were spent in relatively good health. She had a troublesome heart,

but was otherwise fit and well. Mentally, she was as sharp as ever, and spent the majority of her days reading, reflecting, and writing. In her intellectual diary, she quotes Hölderlin's poem "Mnemosyne":

The fruits are ripe, dipped in fire,
Cooked and sampled on earth. And there's a law,
That things crawl off in the manner of snakes,
Prophetically, dreaming on the hills of heaven.
And there is much that needs to be retained,
Like a load of wood on the shoulders.
But the pathways are dangerous.
The captured elements and ancient laws of earth
Run astray like horses. There is a constant yearning
For all that is unconfined. But much needs
To be retained. And loyalty is required,
Yet we mustn't look forwards or backwards.
We should let ourselves be cradled
As if on a boat rocking on a lake.

Mnemosyne is the goddess of memory and the mother of the nine Muses, goddesses of song, music, and poetry. Memory, in other words, is linked to creation — its very origin, in fact. Hannah quoted a few lines from Hölderlin's poem in a letter to Mary, remarking, "In short: remembrance" and discussing the concept of *gravitas* — the weight of the past.

This is the mental space Hannah inhabited during

the years between Heinrich's death and her own. She spent her days writing and her evenings eating dinner with various members of the circle of friends she and Heinrich had been a part of for years. Once a week, she called Mary, who was living in Paris, and wrote numerous letters—not least to Martin.

In late summer 1975, Hannah paid one last visit to Europe. She travelled to the German Literature Archive in Marbach in order to hand over some of the correspondence between herself, Kurt Blumenfeld, and Karl Jaspers. Hannah spent four weeks in Marbach, sorting and archiving the letters. After that, she travelled on to Freiburg. Martin's health was failing, and seeing her former professor and lover looking so wretched left a deep impression on Hannah. She wrote to Mary that she returned home "very depressed. Heidegger is now suddenly really old, very changed from last year, very deaf and remote, unapproachable as I never saw him before. I have been surrounded here for weeks by old people who suddenly got very old."

Hannah was not alone in her concern for Martin; Elfriede, his wife, was also deeply troubled by his faltering health. In their shared worry over the man they both loved, the former rivals found each other, and Hannah travelled back to the United States with a sense of having reconciled with Martin's wife.

ON OCTOBER 14, 1975, Hannah turned sixty-nine, cele-
brating with a big party for new and old friends alike.
She was starting to plan for life after retirement from the
New School, where she had taught for the past decade,
and had decided to leave New York once her time there
was over. Smith College in Northampton, Massachusetts,
had offered her a position as a visiting professor for one
semester, and Hannah had accepted.

Unfortunately, that never came to pass. On Thursday,
December 4, 1975, Hannah died at home in her apartment
on Riverside Drive. Her friends Jeanette and Salo Baron
had gone over for dinner that evening, and they were
chatting in her living room when Hannah was struck
by a sudden coughing fit. She slumped in her armchair
and quickly lost consciousness. The Barons called for a
doctor and for her friend Lotte Kohler, but Hannah never
came around, passing away in her armchair before Lotte
even arrived.

Hannah's funeral took place on December 8 at the
Riverside Memorial Chapel. She had wanted the cere-
mony to be held in the same place as Heinrich's, and
had wished for the same simple service—she was even
buried in the same type of coffin as Heinrich: simple pine,
covered in white roses. The night before the ceremony,
Hannah's closest friends got together to discuss whether
it should involve any Jewish elements, and eventually
settled on a compromise: one of Hannah's younger Israeli
relatives would read a passage from a psalm in Hebrew,

and the Klenborts' son Daniel would read the same psalm in English.

Over three hundred people turned up to pay their respects to Hannah—and, as at Heinrich's funeral, they were given the opportunity to share memories of the deceased. Mary McCarthy and Hans Jonas both spoke, as did Hannah's research assistant Jerome Kohn and publisher William Jovanovich, who described her as "passionate in the way believers in justice can become." Her love of the world was a lifelong driving force, and toward the end this love affair had become less stormy and more harmonious. Hannah died reconciled with the world.

Hannah Arendt, the girl from Königsberg who became one of the most important voices of the twentieth century—a woman who, more than anyone else, personified its violent history—was dead.

What can we learn from Hannah? That we should love the world so much that we believe that change is possible, and that we should never give up.

Acknowledgements

I am indebted to Elisabeth Young-Bruehl's exhausting chronicle of Hannah's life, particularly in the descriptions of her time at the Vélodrome d'Hiver and Camp Gurs, certain anecdotes pertaining to Hannah's many friendships, and details surrounding Hannah and Heinrich's escape from Marseilles.

I have had such invaluable help with my writing from my husband, Erik van der Heeg. Thank you for supporting me with your historical knowledge, your French and German skills, and your sharp eye for stylistic subtleties. I would also like to thank my publisher, Simon Brouwers, who believed in this project and gave me the opportunity and courage to write. Thank you both — without you, this book about Hannah never would have been written.

Ann Heberlein
Malmö, Sweden, March 2020

Index of Key Figures

Below is a list of the people who feature in this book, in alphabetical order.

Walter Benjamin
Born July 15, 1892, in Berlin; died September 26, 1940, in Portbou, Spain. A German philosopher, literary critic, and art critic who grew close to Hannah during her exile in Paris.

Heinrich Blücher
Born January 29, 1889, in Berlin; died October 30, 1970, in New York. Fled Germany for political reasons; an auto-didact in military history and philosophy. Met Hannah in Paris and became her husband.

Kurt Blumenfeld
Born May 29, 1884, in Stuttgart; died May 21, 1963, in Jerusalem, Israel. Secretary General of the World Zionist

Organization. Kurt and Hannah met in Berlin in the 1930s.

Bertolt Brecht
Born February 10, 1898, in Augsburg; died August 14, 1956, in Berlin. German writer, playwright, and director. Became acquainted with Hannah through Heinrich Blücher and Walter Benjamin.

Martin Heidegger
Born in Messkirch, September 26, 1889; died in Freiburg, May 26, 1976. German philosopher whose most famous work is *Being and Time*. Hannah's professor and supervisor in Marburg.

Karl Jaspers
Born February 23, 1883, in Oldenburg; died February 26, 1969, in Basel, Switzerland. German philosopher and psychiatrist who had a great influence on theology, philosophy, and psychology. Hannah's supervisor in Heidelberg.

Hans Jonas
Born May 10, 1903, in Mönchengladbach; died February 5, 1993, in New York. Jewish German philosopher who left Germany for Mandatory Palestine in 1933. Met Hannah as a student in Marburg.

Mary McCarthy

Born June 21, 1912, in Seattle; died October 24, 1989, in New York. American author and writer who met Hannah in New York.

Anne Mendelsohn Weil

Hannah's childhood friend from Königsberg. Doctoral thesis on philosophy from the University of Hamburg. Fled to Paris, like Hannah. Married philosopher Eric Weil. Active member of the French Resistance during the Second World War.

Gershom Scholem

Born December 5, 1897, in Berlin; died February 21, 1982, in Jerusalem. Scholem was a German-Israeli philosopher and historian. Became good friends with Hannah through Walter Benjamin.

Rahel Varnhagen

Born May 19, 1771, in Berlin; died March 7, 1833. German salon hostess, daughter of a Jewish merchant, married to Karl August Varnhagen von Ense. Hannah wrote a biography of her during the 1930s.

Bibliography

WORKS BY HANNAH ARENDT

Denktagebuch 1950–1973. Berlin: Piper Verlag, 2016.

Eichmann in Jerusalem: A Report on the Banality of Evil. New York: Penguin, 2006 [1963].

The Human Condition. Chicago: University of Chicago Press, 2018 [1958]

The Life of the Mind. Vol. 1, *Thinking*. New York: Harcourt Brace Jovanovich, 1978.

The Life of the Mind. Vol. 2, *Willing*. New York: Harcourt Brace Jovanovich, 1978.

Love and Saint Augustine. Edited by Joanna Vecchiarelli Scott and Judith Chelius Stark. Chicago: University of Chicago Press, 1996 [1929].

Mellan det förflutna och framtiden. Göteborg: Daidalos, 2004.

Men in Dark Times. New York: Harcourt, Brace & World, 1968.

On Revolution. New York: Viking Press, 1963.

On Violence. Boston: Houghton Mifflin Harcourt, 1970.

The Origins of Totalitarianism. Boston: Houghton Mifflin Harcourt, 1973 [1951].

Responsibility and Judgment. New York: Schocken Books, 2003.

Rahel Varnhagen: The Life of a Jewish Woman. Translated by Richard and Clara Winston. New York: Harcourt Brace Jovanovich, 1974 [1957].

Rätten till rättigheter: Politiska texter. Stockholm: TankeKraft, 2017.

ARTICLES BY HANNAH ARENDT

"The Concentration Camps." *Partisan Review* 15, no. 7 (July 1948).

"Eichmann in Jerusalem." *Encounter* 22, no. 1 (January 1964).

"The Jew as Pariah: A Hidden Tradition." *Jewish Social Studies* 6, no. 2 (February 1944).

"The Rights of Man: What Are They?" *Modern Review* 3, no. 1 (1949).

"We Refugees." *Menorah Journal* 31, no. 1 (January 1943).

PUBLISHED CORRESPONDENCE OF HANNAH ARENDT

Between Friends: The Correspondence of Hannah Arendt and Mary McCarthy, 1949–1975. Edited by Carol Brightman. New York: Harcourt Brace, 1995.

Correspondence, 1933–1963 [Hannah Arendt and Kurt Blumenfeld]. Paris: Midrash, 1994.

The Correspondence of Hannah Arendt and Gershom Scholem. Edited by Marie Luise Knott. Translated by Anthony David. Chicago: University of Chicago Press, 2017.

Hannah Arendt/Karl Jaspers Correspondence, 1926–1969. Edited by Lotte Köhler and Hans Saner. Translated by Robert and Rita Kimber. New York: Harcourt Brace Jovanovich, 1992.

Letters, 1925–1975 [Hannah Arendt and Martin Heidegger]. Edited by Ursula Ludz. Translated by Andrew Shields. New York: Harcourt, 2004.

Within Four Walls: The Correspondence between Hannah Arendt and Heinrich Blücher, 1936–1968. Edited by Lotte Köhler. Translated by Peter Constantine. New York: Harcourt, 1996.

INTERVIEWS WITH HANNAH ARENDT

Den sista intervjun och andra konversationer: Hannah Arendt. Riga: Sjösala förlag, 2018.

BIOGRAPHIES OF HANNAH ARENDT

Ettinger, Elżbieta. *Hannah Arendt/Martin Heidegger.* Stockholm: Natur och Kultur, 1995.

Kristeva, Julia. *Hannah Arendt.* Translated by Ross Guberman. New York: Columbia University Press, 2001.

Young-Bruehl, Elisabeth. *Hannah Arendt: For Love of the World.* New Haven and London: Yale University Press, 1982.

OTHER LITERATURE

Améry, Jean. *On Aging: Revolt and Resignation*. Translated by John D. Barlow. Bloomington and Indianapolis: Indiana University Press, 1994.

Améry, Jean. *On Suicide: A Discourse on Voluntary Death*. Translated by John D. Barlow. Bloomington: Indiana University Press, 1999.

Aristotle. *The Nichomachean Ethics*. London: Penguin, 2004.

Aristotle. *The Politics*. London: Penguin, 1981.

Baudrillard, Jean. *Seduction*. Translated by Brian Singer. New York: St. Martin's Press, 1990.

Bauman, Zygmunt. *Arbete, konsumtion och den nya fattigdomen*. Göteborg: Daidalos, 1999.

Becker, Ernest. *The Denial of Death*. New York: Free Press, 1973.

de Beauvoir, Simone. *The Coming of Age*. Translated by Patrick O'Brian. New York: W.W. Norton & Company, 1996.

de Beauvoir, Simone. *Force of Circumstance*. Translated by Richard Howard. London: Weidenfeld and Nicolson, 1966.

Benhabib, Seyla. *Exile, Statelessness, and Migration: Playing Chess with History from Hannah Arendt to Isaiah Berlin*. Princeton, NJ: Princeton University Press, 2018.

Bettelheim, Bruno. *Surviving and Other Essays*. New York: Knopf, 1979.

Booth, Wayne. *The Company We Keep: An Ethics of Fiction*. Oakland: University of California Press, 1988.

Bourdieu, Pierre. *Language and Symbolic Power*. Edited by John Thompson. Translated by Gino Raymond and Matthew Adamson. Cambridge, MA: Harvard University Press, 1991.

Browning, Christopher. *Helt vanliga män*. Stockholm: Norstedts, 2006.

Christie, Nils. *Fangevoktere i konsentrasjonsleire*. Oslo: Universitetsförlaget, 1972.

Drakulic, Slavenka. *Inte en fluga förnär*. Stockholm: Norstedts, 2004.

Frankl, Viktor. *Man's Search for Meaning*. London: Rider/Ebury Press, 2004.

García Márquez, Gabriel. *Living to Tell the Tale*. Translated by Edith Grossman. New York: Penguin, 2008.

Glover, Jonathan. *Humanity: A Moral History of the Twentieth Century*. New Haven, CT: Yale University Press, 2000.

Hampton, Jean, and Jeffrie G. Murphy. *Forgiveness and Mercy*. Cambridge, U.K.: Cambridge University Press, 1988.

Hilberg, Raul. *The Destruction of the European Jews*. New Haven, CT: Yale University Press, 2003.

Heidegger, Martin. *Schwarze Hefte*. Frankfurt: Verlag Vittorio Klostermann, 2019.

Holmgren, Margaret. "Forgiveness and the Intrinsic Value of Persons." *American Philosophical Quarterly* 30, no. 4 (October 1993).

Jankélévitch, Vladimir. *La Mort*. Paris: Flammarion, 1966.

Jaspers, Karl. *Psychologie der Weltanschauungen*. Berlin: Springer, 1919.

Kant, Immanuel. *Grundläggning av sedernas metafysik.* Stockholm: Björck & Börjesson, 1920.

Kant, Immanuel. *Lectures on Ethics.* Translated by Louis Infield. Gloucester, MA: Peter Smith, 1963.

Kant, Immanuel. *Kritik av det rena förnuftet.* Stockholm: Thales, 2004.

Kierkegaard, Søren. *Antingen – eller: Ett livsfragment.* Stockholm: Wahlström & Widstrand, 1964.

Kristofersen, Knut. *Heydrich – Förintelsens arkitekt.* Stockholm: Albert Bonniers Förlag, 2009.

Kyrklund, Willy. *Om godheten.* Stockholm: Alba, 1988.

Levinas, Emmanuel. *Humanism of the Other.* Translated by Nidra Poller. Urbana, IL: University of Illinois Press, 2003.

Machiavelli, Niccolò. *Fursten.* Stockholm: Natur & Kultur, 2009.

Manz, Bruno. *Fångad av hakkorset: Nazist och soldat i tredje riket.* Lund: Historiska media, 2008.

Milgram, Stanley. *Obedience to Authority: An Experimental View.* New York: Harper & Row, 1973.

Monroe, Kristen Renwick. *The Heart of Altruism: Perceptions of a Common Humanity.* Princeton, NJ: Princeton University Press, 1996.

Murphy, Jeffrie G. *Getting Even: Forgiveness and Its Limits.* New York: Oxford University Press, 2003.

Nietzsche, Friedrich. *Beyond Good and Evil: Prelude to a Philosophy of the Future.* Translated by Walter Kaufmann. New York: Vintage Books, 1989.

Nietzsche, Friedrich. *On the Genealogy of Morals*. Translated by Walter Kaufmann. New York: Vintage Books, 1969.

Nietzsche, Friedrich. *The Will to Power*. Translated by Walter Kaufmann and R. J. Hollingdale. New York: Vintage Books, 1968.

Nussbaum, Martha. *Love's Knowledge: Essays on Philosophy and Literature*. Oxford: Oxford University Press, 1992.

Oliner, Samuel P., and Pearl M. Oliner. *The Altruistic Personality: Rescuers of Jews in Nazi Europe*. New York: Free Press, 1988.

Pico della Mirandola, Giovanni. *Oration on the Dignity of Man*. Cambridge, U.K.: Cambridge University Press, 2012.

Plato. *The Republic*. London: Penguin, 2007.

Russell, Bertrand. *Marriage and Morals*. New York: Sun Dial Press, 1938.

Russell, Dora. *The Right to Be Happy*. New York: Harper & Brothers, 1927.

Scruton, Roger. *Sexual Desire: A Moral Philosophy of the Erotic*. New York: Free Press, 1986.

Sereny, Gitta. *Albert Speer och sanningen*. Stockholm: Bonnier Alba, 1997.

Sereny, Gitta. *Vid avgrunden: Från barmhärtighetsmord till folkförintelse*. Stockholm: Ordfront, 2000.

Shklar, Judith N. *Ordinary Vices*. Cambridge, MA: Belknap Press, 1984.

Weber, Max. *Ekonomi och samhälle: Förståendesociologins grunder*. Lund: Argos, 1995.

Welzer, Harald. *Gärningsmän: Hur helt vanliga människor blir mass – mördare.* Göteborg: Daidalos, 2007.

Wiesenthal, Simon. *The Sunflower: On the Possibilities and Limits of Forgiveness.* Paris: Opera Mundi, 1969.

Zimbardo, Philip. *The Lucifer Effect: Understanding How Good People Turn Evil.* London: Rider/Ebury Press, 2007.

Permissions

Permission is gratefully acknowledged to reprint excerpts from the following:

Men in Dark Times (1968), *The Origins of Totalitarianism* (1973), and *The Life of the Mind* (1978) by Hannah Arendt, courtesy of Houghton Mifflin Harcourt.

Eichmann in Jerusalem by Hannah Arendt copyright © 1963, 1964 by Hannah Arendt; copyright renewed © 1991, 1992 by Lotte Kohler. Used by permission of Viking Books, an imprint of Penguin Publishing Group, a division of Penguin Random House LLC. All rights reserved.

The Human Condition by Hannah Arendt (2018), courtesy of University of Chicago Press.

Within Four Walls, edited by Lotte Köhler and translated by Peter Constantine (1996), courtesy of Houghton Mifflin Harcourt and Piper Verlag.

Letters: 1925–1975, edited by Ursula Ludz and translated by Andrew Shields (2004), courtesy of Houghton Mifflin Harcourt and Verlag Vittorio Klostermann.

DR. ANN HEBERLEIN is the bestselling author of more than a dozen books, including *A Little Book on Evil*, *A Good Life*, and the autobiographical *I Don't Want to Die, I Just Don't Want to Live*, which has sold hundreds of thousands of copies, been translated into multiple languages, and been dramatized and mounted on several stages. In 2018, Heberlein debuted as a fiction writer with the novel *Everything Is Going to Be All Right*. Heberlein has researched and taught at the Department of Practical Philosophy at Stockholm University and at the Faculty of Theology, Lund University.

ALICE MENZIES is a literary translator from the Swedish and has translated works by several contemporary Swedish writers, including Fredrik Backman and Sofia Lundberg. She lives in London, U.K.